YOUR GOD IS TOO SMALL

BY J. B. PHILLIPS

LETTERS TO YOUNG CHURCHES
  A translation of the New Testament Epistles

THE GOSPELS *translated into Modern English*

YOUR GOD IS TOO SMALL

YOUR GOD IS TOO SMALL

by

J. B. PHILLIPS

THE MACMILLAN COMPANY—NEW YORK

Fifth printing, 1954

CONTENTS

iv
CONTENTS

INTRODUCTORY

No ONE is ever really at ease in facing what we call "life" and "death" without a religious faith. The trouble with many people today is that they have not found a God big enough for modern needs. While their experience of life has grown in a score of directions, and their mental horizons have been expanded to the point of bewilderment by world events and by scientific discoveries, their ideas of God have remained largely static. It is obviously impossible for an adult to worship the conception of God that exists in the mind of a child of Sunday-school age, unless he is prepared to deny his own experience of life. If, by a great effort of will, he does do this he will always be secretly afraid lest some new truth may expose the juvenility of his faith. And it will always be by such an effort that he either worships or serves a God who is really too small to command his adult loyalty and co-operation.

It often appears to those outside the Churches that this is precisely the attitude of Christian people. If they are not strenuously defending an outgrown conception of God, then they are cherishing a hothouse God who could only exist between the pages of the Bible or inside the four walls of a church. Therefore to join in with the worship of a church would be to become a party to a piece of mass-hypocrisy and to buy a sense of security at the price of the sense of truth, and many men of goodwill will not consent to such a transaction.

It cannot be denied that there is a little truth in this criticism. There are undoubtedly professing Christians with childish conceptions of God which could not stand up to the winds of real life for five minutes. But Christians are by no means always unintelligent, naïve, or immature. Many of them hold a faith in God that has been both purged and developed by the strains and perplexities of modern times, as well as by a small but by no means negligible direct experience of God Himself. They have seen enough to know that God is immeasurably "bigger" than our forefathers imagined, and modern scientific discovery only confirms their belief that man has only just begun to comprehend the incredibly complex Being who is behind what we call "life."

Many men and women today are living, often with inner dissatisfaction, without any faith in God at all. This is not because they are particularly wicked or selfish or, as the old-fashioned would say, "godless," but because they have not found with their adult minds a God big enough to "account for" life, big enough to "fit in with" the new scientific age, big enough to command their highest admiration and respect, and consequently their willing co-operation.

It is the purpose of this book to attempt two things:

first to expose the inadequate conceptions of God which still linger unconsciously in many minds, and which prevent our catching a glimpse of the true God; and secondly to suggest ways in which we can find the real God for ourselves. If it is true that there is Someone in charge of the whole mystery of life and death, we can hardly expect to escape a sense of futility and frustration until we begin to see what He is like and what His purposes are.

PART ONE—*DESTRUCTIVE*

UNREAL GODS

I. RESIDENT POLICEMAN

To MANY people conscience is almost all that they have by way of knowledge of God. This still small voice which makes them feel guilty and unhappy before, during, or after wrong-doing, is God speaking to them. It is this which, to some extent at least, controls their conduct. It is this which impels them to shoulder the irksome duty and choose the harder path.

Now no serious advocate of a real adult religion would deny the function of conscience, or deny that its voice may at least give some inkling of the moral order that lies behind the obvious world in which we live. Yet to make conscience into God is a highly dangerous thing to do. For one thing, as we shall see in a moment, conscience is by no means an infallible guide; and for another it is extremely unlikely that we shall ever be moved to worship, love, and serve, a nagging inner voice that at worst spoils our pleasure

9

and at best keeps us rather negatively on the path of virtue.

Conscience can be so easily perverted or morbidly developed in the sensitive person, and so easily ignored and silenced by the insensitive, that it makes a very unsatisfactory god. For while it is probably true that every normal person has an embryo moral sense by which he can distinguish right from wrong, the development, non-development, or perversion of that sense is largely a question of upbringing, training, and propaganda.

As an example of the first, we may suppose a child to be brought up by extremely strict vegetarian parents. If the child, now grown adolescent, attempts to eat meat he will in all probability suffer an extremely bad attack of "conscience." If he is brought up to regard certain legitimate pleasures as "worldly" and reprehensible he will similarly suffer pangs of conscience if he seeks the forbidden springs of recreation. The voice will no doubt sound like the voice of God; but it is only the voice of the early upbringing which has conditioned his moral sense.

As an example of the second influence on the moral sense, we may take a "sportsman" who has been trained from his youth that it is "wrong" to shoot a sitting bird. Should he do so, even accidentally, he will undoubtedly feel a sense of shame and wrongdoing; though to shoot a bird flying twenty yards in front of the muzzle of his gun will not produce any sense of guilt. His conscience has been artificially trained, and it is thus that "taboos" are maintained among the civilized and uncivilized alike.

Any sport, and indeed many professions, can provide abundant instances of the moral sense trained to feel that certain things are "not done." The feeling of guilt and failure produced by doing the forbidden thing may be quite false, and is in many cases quite disproportionate to the actual moral wrong, if indeed there be any.

As an example of the third way in which the moral sense may be conditioned, we may take the way in which public propaganda influenced those of sensitive conscience during the last World War. It was perfectly possible for an extreme sense of guilt to be aroused if paper were burned (because propaganda had said that it should be salvaged), or if a journey by rail were undertaken (did not propaganda shout on every hand, "Is your journey really necessary?").

In Nazi Germany, of course, propaganda as a weapon to pervert the moral sense became a fine art. It soon seemed, for example, a positive duty to hate the Jews, and a good Nazi would doubtless have suffered pangs of conscience if he had been kind to one of the despised race.

These examples may be enough to show the unwisdom of calling conscience, God. Obviously this invaluable moral sense can be rightly trained and even rightly influenced by propaganda, provided we can be sure what we mean by right. But to define that word we need to discover God—for without God no one has any authority to advance in support of his ideas of "right," except his own moral sense. Unless there is a God by whom "right" and "wrong" can be reliably assessed, moral judgements can be no more than opinion, influenced by upbringing, training, and propaganda.

In this country of England, centuries of Christian tradition have so permeated our life that we forget how our moral sense has been conditioned by a dilute, but genuine, Christianity. Our attitude toward women and children, toward the weak and helpless, or toward animals, for instance, is not nearly so "innate" as we think. It was a shock to many men of our armed forces who were stationed abroad during the last war to discover how poor and blind was the moral sense in these directions in countries which had no Christian tradition. No doubt many put this down to the fact that the inhabitants of these countries had the misfortune not to be English! It would be truer to say that they had had the misfortune not to have had their moral sense stimulated and developed by Christian upbringing, training, and propaganda.

Many moralists, both Christian and non-Christian, have pointed out the decline in our moral sense observed in recent years. It is at least arguable that this is almost wholly due to the decline in the first-hand absorption of Christian ideals. True Christianity has never had a serious rival in the training of the moral sense which exists in ordinary people.

Yet there are many, even among professing Christians, who are made miserable by a morbidly developed conscience, which they quite wrongly consider to be the voice of God. Many a housewife overdrives herself to please some inner voice that demands perfection. The voice may be her own demands or the relics of childhood training, but it certainly is not likely to be the voice of the Power behind the Universe.

On the other hand, the middle-aged business man who has long ago taught his conscience to come to heel may persuade himself that he is a good-living man. He may even say, with some pride, that he would never do anything against his conscience. But it is impossible to believe that the feeble voice of the half-blind thing which he calls a conscience is in any real sense the voice of God.

Surely neither the hectically over-developed nor the falsely-trained, nor the moribund conscience can ever be regarded as God, or even part of Him. For if it is, God can be made to appear to the sensitive an over-exacting tyrant, and to the insensitive a comfortable accommodating "Voice Within" which would never interfere with a man's pleasure.

II. PARENTAL HANGOVER

MANY PSYCHOLOGISTS assure us that the trend of the whole of a man's life is largely determined by his attitude in early years toward his parents. Many normal people, with happy childhoods behind them, may scoff at this, but nevertheless the clinics and consulting-rooms of psychiatrists are thronged with those whose inner lives were distorted in early childhood by their relationship toward their parents. Quite a lot of ordinary people, who would never dream of turning to psychiatry, nevertheless have an abnormal fear of authority, or of a dominating personality of either sex, which could without much difficulty be traced back to the tyranny of a parent. Conversely there are many who would be insulted by the name "neurotic," but who nevertheless are imperfectly adjusted to life, and whose inner sense of superiority makes them difficult to work or live with. It would again not be difficult to trace in their history a childhood of spoiling and indulgence, in which the child's natural self-love was never checked or directed outward into interest in other people. The child is truly "the father of the man."

But what has this to do with an inadequate conception of God? This, that the early conception of God is almost invariably founded upon the child's idea of his father. If he is lucky enough to have a good father this is all to the good, provided of course that the conception of God grows with the rest of personality. But if the child is afraid (or, worse still, afraid and feeling guilty because he *is* afraid) of his own father, the chances are that his Father in Heaven will appear to him a fearful Being. Again, if he is lucky, he will outgrow this conception, and indeed differentiate between his early "fearful" idea and his later mature conception. But many are not able to outgrow the sense of guilt and fear, and in adult years are still obsessed with it, although it has actually nothing to do with their real relationship with the living God. It is nothing more than a parental hang-over. Many priests and ministers with some knowl-edge of psychology will have met the person abnor-mally afraid of God, and will have been able to recognize the psychological, rather than the religious, significance of the fear. Some of them will have had the joy of seeing the religious faith blossom out into joy and confidence, when the psychological dishar-mony has been analysed and resolved. To describe that process would be outside the scope of this book, but it is worth observing for the sake of those who may possibly suffer from an irrational fear of, or violent revolt from, the idea of God that the root of their trouble is probably not their "sin" or their "rebelliousness," but what they felt toward their parents when they were very young.

It is interesting, though rather pathetic, to note here that the success of a certain type of Christianity depends almost wholly on this sense of guilt. For the "gospel" will be accepted only by those in whom the sense of guilt can be readily awakened or stimulated. Indeed, missioners of this type of Christianity (flying incidentally in the face of Christ's own example) will go all out to induce and foster "conviction of sin" in their hearers. The results of such efforts are usually small, a fact attributed by the missioner to the hardness of the hearts of his hearers. It is really due to the healthy reaction against artificial guilt-injection possessed by all but those few whose unhappy childhood has left them peculiarly open to this form of spiritual assault.

This, of course, is not to deny the fact of human sin or the necessity of divine forgiveness. There is a real "conviction of sin" which is quite different in quality from that produced by high-pressure evangelism. These matters must be considered further in a later chapter. What we are concerned in establishing here is that the conception of God which is based upon a fear-relationship in childhood is not a satisfactory foundation for an adult Christianity. Much of the fear of God which characterized an earlier generation was the fruit of fear of parents, and it was not difficult to arouse a sense of sinfulness or fear of hell in those whose childhood was highly coloured by memories of guilt, shame, and the fear of punishment.

So firmly established in the minds of some non-

Christian psychologists is this connexion between the father-image of early childhood and the later conception of God, that they will go so far as to say that all religion is regressive, that is, an attempt to return to the dependence of childhood by clinging to the idea of a parent. It can hardly be denied that this is true in some cases, but it is manifestly nonsense in the case of some of the greatest and maturest personalities that the world has seen who have held a firm belief in a Personal God. Moreover it is the experience of Christians who have been "psychoanalysed" that, although the process disentangles from their faith something that is childish and even sentimental, yet there remains a hard core of thoroughly satisfactory adult conviction and faith.

But surely, it may be objected, Christ Himself taught us to regard God as a Father. Are we to reject His own analogy? Of course not, so long as we remember that it *is* an analogy. When Christ taught His disciples to regard God as their Father in Heaven He did not mean that their idea of God must necessarily be based upon their ideas of their own fathers. For all we know there may have been many of His hearers whose fathers were unjust, tyrannical, stupid, conceited, feckless, or indulgent. It is the *relationship* that Christ is stressing. The intimate love for, and interest in, his son possessed by a good earthly father represents to men a relationship that they can understand, even if they themselves are fatherless! The same sort

of relationship, Christ is saying, can be reliably reck-
oned upon by man in his dealings with God.

There are Christians who do not appear to understand this properly. Because Christ said that men
must become "as little children" (i.e. repudiate all
the sham, compromise, and cynicism, of adulthood)
before they could play their part in His Kingdom
with simplicity and sincerity, some have supposed
that He places a premium upon human immaturity.
It is ludicrous to suppose that any sensible God can
wish adult men and women to crawl about in spiritual rompers in order to preserve a rather sentimental
Father-child relationship. Indeed, experience shows
that it is only the mature Christian man who can
begin to see a little of the "size" of his Father. He
may previously have thought that the comparison of
the relationship between the toddler and his grown-up
father with his own relationship toward God was
rather an exaggeration of the gulf, in intelligence at
least. But in his growing maturity he is likely to see
that Christ, in His kindness of heart, has certainly not
exaggerated the awe-inspiring disparity between man
and God.

To have a God, then, who is as much, or more, our
superior than we are the superior of an infant child
crawling on the hearthrug, is not to hold a childish
concept of God, but rather the reverse. It is only
when we limit the mind's stirrings after its Maker by
imposing upon it half-forgotten images of our own

earthly parents, that we grow frustrated in spirit and wonder why for us the springs of worship and love do not flow. We must leave behind "parental hangover" if we are to find a "big enough" God.

III. GRAND OLD MAN

IT IS SAID that some Sunday-school children were once asked to write down their ideas as to what God was like. The answers, with few exceptions, began something like this: "God is a very old gentleman living in Heaven . . ."! Whether this story is true or not, there is no doubt that in many children's minds God is an "old" person. This is partly due, of course, to the fact that a child's superiors are always "old" to him and God must therefore be the "oldest" of all. Moreover, a child is so frequently told that he will be able to do such-and-such a thing or understand such-and-such a matter "when he is older," that it is only natural that the Source of all strength and wisdom must seem to him very old indeed. In addition to this his mind has quite probably been filled with stories of God's activities which happened "long ago." He is in consequence quite likely to feel, and even visualize, God as someone very old.

It may be argued that there is no particular harm in this. Since the child must adapt himself to an adult world there can be nothing wrong in his concept of an "old" God. But there is nevertheless a very real danger that the child will imagine this God not merely as "old," but as "old-fashioned"; and may indeed be so impressed with God's actions in "times of old" that he may fail to grasp the idea of God operating with unimpaired energy in the present and leading forward into a hopeful future.

But even if it be admitted that to visualize God as "old" will do a child no harm, the persistence of the idea of childhood beneath the surface of the mind may well make it difficult to develop and hold an adequate idea of God in later years. In order to test whether this "old-fashioned" concept was persisting in modern young people, a simple psychological test was recently applied to a mixed group of older adolescents. They were asked to answer, without reflection, the question: "Do you think God understands radar?" In nearly every case the reply was "No," followed of course by a laugh, as the conscious mind realized the absurdity of the answer. But, simple as this test was, it was quite enough to show that *at the back of their minds* these youngsters held an idea of God quite inadequate for modern days. Subsequent discussion showed plainly that while "they had not really thought much about it," they had freely to admit that the idea of God, absorbed some years before, existed in quite a separate compartment from their modern experience, knowledge, and outlook. It was as though they were revering the memory of a Grand Old Man, who was a great power in His day, but who could not possibly be expected to keep pace with modern progress!

There are probably many people today with a similar "split" in their mental conceptions. The "Grand Old Man" is treated with reverence and respect—look what a help He was to our forefathers! —but He can hardly be expected to cope with the complexities and problems of life today! If the absurdity of this "split" makes us laugh, so much the better.

There is much in our Churches and religious teaching generally that tends to encourage the "old-fashioned" concept. The Bible is read in beautiful but old-fashioned language, as a rule. Our services are often entirely conducted in a form of language that no one uses today. We address God in our prayers in the archaic second person singular—and these prayers themselves often give the impression of being cast in a form that the Grand Old Man can both understand and approve. Our hymns, with some notable exceptions, often express a Victorian and very rarely a "big enough" idea of God. To appreciate their true value they should be read aloud in cold blood and dissociated from the well-loved tunes. At baptism, matrimony, and burial, we continue to use language which ordinary people can hardly understand, but which they feel vaguely is old-fashioned and out of touch with their actual lives. They respect the Grand Old Man and His peculiarities, but they feel no inclination to worship Him as the living God.

Sermons and addresses again and again are stuffed with religious jargon and technical terms which strike no answering chord in the modern heart. It is no doubt a joy to the preacher to know that he is not only serving the same God as the saints of the past, but even using the time-honoured phrases which meant so much to them. But to his modern hearers (if they can be got within earshot!) he will only seem to be in love with the past. His words may have beauty and dignity, but it is the beauty and dignity of a past age; and his message often appears to be wholly irrelevant to the issues of today.

Where people have been "conditioned" by a Christian upbringing the worship of the average Church may to some extent satisfy. In all probability they are, through long practice, "translating" as they go along. But to the average young person of today, brought up without such background, conventional Christian worship will appear reactionary and old-fashioned, and such ideas of God as may be stimulated in his mind will be of the Grand-Old-Man type. His pressing, though inarticulate, need is not for the God of the ancient Hebrews, nor the God of the early Church, nor the God of Victorian England, but the God of the Atomic Age—the God of Energy and Wisdom and Love *today*.

Clever people often scathingly criticize the youth of today for having "no historic sense." But surely that is hardly to be wondered at. So great and far-reaching have been the changes in modern life that the young man of today cannot see any but the slenderest connexion between what appears to him the slow simple and secure life of a bygone generation and the highly-complex fast-moving life of the world today. The historic sense is often the fruit of maturity, and while an experienced Christian may be glad to think that he is worshipping the same God as did Abraham, Moses, David, and the saints of the Christian Church, the young man of today, even if he knows who Abraham, Moses, and David were, will be quite unmoved by the historical connexion. His clamant need is for an adequate God of Today; the historic sense may well come later.

It will be necessary, as we shall see in a later chapter, to look back into human history at the actual events which are the foundation of the Christian view of God. But it will be just as necessary to return, armed with the essential historical facts, to the modern world. No figure in history, however splendid and memorable, can possibly satisfy the mind which is seeking the living contemporary God.

IV. MEEK-AND-MILD

IT IS A thousand pities that the word "child" has so few words that rhyme with it appropriate for a hymn. But for this paucity of language we might have been spared the couplet that hundreds of thousands must have learned in their childhood:

> Gentle Jesus, meek and mild,
> Look upon a little child.

But perhaps it was not the stringencies of verse-making that led the writer to apply the word "mild" to Jesus Christ, for here it is in another children's hymn and this time at the beginning of the line:

> Christian children all must be
> Mild, obedient, good as He.

Why *"mild"*? Of all the epithets that could be applied to Christ this seems one of the least appropriate. For what does "mild," as applied to a person, conjure up to our minds? Surely a picture of someone who wouldn't so "bo" to the proverbial goose; someone who would let sleeping dogs lie and avoid trouble wherever possible; someone of a placid temperament who is almost a stranger to the passions of red-blooded humanity; someone who is a bit of a nonentity, both uninspired and uninspiring.

This word "mild" is apparently deliberately used to describe a man who did not hesitate to challenge and expose the hypocrisies of the religious people of His day: a man who had such "personality" that He walked unscathed through a murderous crowd; a man so far from being a nonentity that He was regarded by the authorities as a public danger; a man who could be moved to violent anger by shameless exploitation or by smug complacent orthodoxy; a man of such courage that He deliberately walked to what He knew would mean death, despite the earnest pleas of well-meaning friends! Mild! What a word to use for a personality whose challenge and strange attractiveness nineteen centuries have by no means exhausted. Jesus Christ might well be called "meek," in the sense of being selfless and humble and utterly devoted to what He considered right, whatever the personal cost; but "mild," never!

Yet it is this fatal combination of "meek and mild" which has been so often, and is even now, applied to Him. We can hardly be surprised if children feel fairly soon that they have outgrown the "tender Shepherd" and find their heroes elsewhere.

But if the impression of a soft and sentimental Jesus has been made (supported, alas, all too often by sugary hymns and pretty religious pictures), the harm is not over when the adolescent rejects the soft and childish conception. There will probably linger at the back of his mind an idea that Christ and the Christian religion is a soft and sentimental thing which has nothing to do with the workaday world. For there is no doubt that this particular "inadequate god," the mild and soft and sentimental, still exists in many adult minds. Indeed the very word "Jesus" conjures up to many people a certain embarrassing sweet tenderness (which incidentally could easily be put in its proper place by an intelligent adult reading of the Gospels). The appeal of this sickly-sweet figure, or of those whose methods are founded on such a concept, is rightly regarded by normal people as "below the belt." But in fact there is no connexion between what has been rudely called the "creeping-Jesus" method and the life and character of the real Christ. The real beauty, love, and tenderness of Christ's character are not, of course, being denied or minimized, but when one characteristic is caricatured at the expense of all the others we get a grotesque distortion which can only appeal to the morbidly sentimental.

The danger of the "meek-and-mild" idea is two-fold. First, since Christians believe that the character of Christ is an accurate depiction in time and space of the Character of the Eternal Deity, it is apt to lead to a conception of God that is woolly and sentimental. We shall have more to say of this in a later chapter, and we will merely point out here the impossibility of a mature adult's feeling constrained to worship a god whose emotional equipment is less developed than his own. The second danger is that since it is axiomatic with Christians that God is love, this most terrible and beautiful of all the virtues becomes debased and cheapened.

It would seem that the "meek-and-mild" conception of the Deity could be readily seen through, yet experience shows that it is operating beneath the conscious level of many Christian minds, particularly in those whose childhood has been coloured by a sentimental attitude toward "the Lord Jesus." Such people find their actions, and even their thoughts, inhibited by a false consideration of what is "loving." They can neither use their critical faculties nor speak the plain truth nor meet their fellows "naturally" for fear they sin against the meek-and-mild god. To non-Christians they thus appear unreal or even as hypocrites, while the "love" they attempt to exhibit toward others is all too often a pathetic travesty of the real thing. For, like other sentimentalists, the meek-and-mild god is in reality cruel; and those whose lives have been governed by him from early childhood have never been allowed to develop their real selves. Forced to be "loving," they have never been free to love.

There is a further offshoot of the worship of this false god which must be mentioned. It is the sentimental Christian ideal of "saintliness." We hear, or read, of someone who was "a real saint: he never saw any harm in anyone and never spoke a word against anyone all his life." If this really is Christian saintliness then Jesus Christ was no saint. It is true that He taught men not to sit in judgement upon one another, but He never suggested that they should turn a blind eye to evil or pretend that other people were faultless. He Himself indulged no roseate visions of human nature: He "knew what was in man," as St. John tersely puts it. Nor can we imagine Him either

using or advocating the invariable use of "loving"
words. To speak the truth was obviously to Him more
important than to make His hearers comfortable:
though, equally obviously, His genuine love for men
gave Him tact, wisdom, and sympathy. He was Love
in action, but He was not meek and mild.

V. ABSOLUTE PERFECTION

OF ALL THE false gods there is probably no greater
nuisance in the spiritual world than the "god of one
hundred per cent." For he is plausible. It can so easily
be argued that since God is Perfection, and since
He asks the complete loyalty of His creatures, then
the best way of serving, pleasing, and worshipping
Him is to set up absolute one-hundred-per-cent standards and see to it that we obey them. After all, did
not Christ say, "Be ye perfect"?

This one-hundred-per-cent standard is a real men-
ace to Christians of various schools of thought, and
has led quite a number of sensitive conscientious
people to what is popularly called a "nervous break-
down." And it has taken the joy and spontaneity out
of the Christian lives of many more who dimly realize
that what was meant to be a life of "perfect freedom"
has become an anxious slavery.

It is probably only people of certain backgrounds
and temperaments who will find the "one-hundred-
per-cent god" a terrible tyrant. A young athletic

extravert may talk glibly enough of being "one-hundred-per-cent pure, honest, loving, and unselfish." But being what he is, he hasn't the faintest conception of what "one hundred per cent" means. He has neither the mental equipment nor the imagination to begin to grasp what perfection really is. He is not the type to analyse his own motives, or build up an artificial conscience to supervise his own actions, or be confronted by a terrifying mental picture of what one-hundred-per-cent perfection literally means in relation to his own life and effort. What *he* means by "one-hundred-per-cent pure, honest, etc." is just as pure and honest as he sincerely knows how. And that is a very different matter.

But the conscientious, sensitive, imaginative person who is somewhat lacking in self-confidence and inclined to introspection, will find one-hundred-per-cent perfection truly terrifying. The more he thinks of it as God's demand the more guilty and miserable he will become, and he cannot see any way out of his impasse. If he reduces the one hundred per cent he is betraying his own spiritual vision, and the very God who might have helped him is the Author (so he imagines) of the terrific demands! No wonder he often "breaks down." The tragedy is often that the "one-hundred-per-cent god" is introduced into the life of the sensitive by the comparatively insensitive, who literally cannot imagine the harm they are doing.

What is the way out? The words of Christ, "Learn

of Me," provide the best clue. Some of our modern
enthusiastic Christians of the hearty type tend to regard Christianity as a performance. But it still is, as
it was originally, a way of living, and in no sense a
performance acted for the benefit of the surrounding
world. To "learn" implies growth; implies the making and correcting of mistakes; implies a steady
upward progress toward an ideal. The "perfection"
to which Christ commands men to progress is this
ideal. The modern high-pressure Christian of certain
circles would like to impose perfection of one hundred per cent as a set of rules to be immediately
enforced, instead of as a shining ideal to be faithfully pursued. His short cut, in effect, makes the
unimaginative satisfied before he ought to be and
drives the imaginative to despair. Such a distortion
of Christian truth could not possibly originate from
the One who said His "yoke was easy" and His
"burden light," nor by His follower St. Paul, who
declared after many years' experience that he "pressed
toward the mark not as though he had already at-
tained or were already perfect."

Yet even to people who have not been driven to
distraction by "one-hundred-per-cent" Christianity,
the same fantasy of perfection may be masquerading
in their minds as God. Because it is a fantasy it produces paralysis and a sense of frustration. The true
ideal, as we shall see later, stimulates, encourages, and
produces likeness to itself.

If we believe in God, we must naturally believe that He is Perfection. But we must not think, to speak colloquially, that He cannot therefore be interested in anything less than perfection. (If that were so, the human race would be in poor case!)

Christians may truthfully say that it is God's "ambition" to possess the wholehearted love and loyalty of His children, but to imagine that He will have no dealings with them until they are prepared to give Him perfect devotion is just another manifestation of the "god of one hundred per cent." After all, who, apart from the very smug and complacent, would claim that they were wholly "surrendered" or "converted" to love? And who would deny the father's interest in the prodigal son when his Spiritual Index was at a very low figure indeed?

God is truly Perfection, but He is no Perfectionist, and one hundred per cent is not God.

VI. HEAVENLY BOSOM

THE CRITICS of the Christian religion have often contended that a religious faith is a form of psychological "escapism." A man, they say, finding the problems and demands of adult life too much for him will attempt to return to the comfort and dependence of childhood by picturing for himself a loving parent, whom he calls God. It must be admitted that there is a good deal of ammunition ready to hand for such an attack, and the first verse of a well-known and well-loved hymn provides an obvious example—

> Jesu, Lover of my soul,
>   Let me to Thy bosom fly,
> While the nearer waters roll,
>   While the tempest still is high:
> Hide me, O my Saviour, hide,
>   Till the storm of life be past;
> Safe into the haven guide,
>   O receive my soul at last.

Here, if the words are taken at their face value, is sheer escapism, a deliberate desire to be hidden safe away until the storm and stress of life is over, and no explaining away by lovers of the hymn can alter its plain sense. It can hardly be denied that if this is true Christianity then the charge of "escapism," of emotional immaturity and childish regression, must be frankly conceded. But although this "God of escape" is quite common the true Christian course is set in a very different direction. No one would accuse its Founder of immaturity in insight, thought, teaching, or conduct, and the history of the Christian Church provides thousands of examples of timid half-developed personalities who have not only found in their faith what the psychologists call integration, but have coped with difficulties and dangers in a way that makes any gibe of "escapism" plainly ridiculous.

Yet is there in Christianity a legitimate element of what the inimical might call escapism?

The authentic Christian tradition, and particularly the biographies of those who might be considered in the front rank of Christian "saints," show that throughout the ages heroic men and women have found in God their "refuge" as well as their "strength." It would be absurd to think that people of such spiritual stature were all under the influence of a childish regression, and we are forced to look farther for the explanation.

It has been well said by several modern psychologists that it is not the outward storms and stresses of life that defeat and disrupt personality, but its inner conflicts and miseries. If a man is happy and stable at heart, he can normally cope, even with zest, with difficulties that lie outside his personality. For example, a man who is happily married and can return daily to a happy home is not likely to be defeated by outward trials and strains. But the same man could quite easily go to pieces and find life altogether too much for him if his marriage, for instance, were to collapse—if in fact the centre of his operations were destroyed.

Now Christians maintain that it is precisely this secure centre which faith in God provides. The genuine Christian can and does venture out into all kinds of exacting and even perilous activities, but all the time he knows that he has a completely stable and unchanging centre of operations to which he can return for strength, refreshment, and recuperation. In that sense he does "escape" to God, though he does not avoid the duties or burdens of life. His very "escape" fits him for the day-to-day engagement with life's strains and difficulties.

But having said this—for it must be said—about the legitimate periodical retirement of the Christian into conscious contact with his God, let us return to the inadequate idea of God which is all too common with certain people—the god in whose bosom we can hide "till the storm of life be past."

Those who are actually, though unconsciously, looking for a father- or mother-substitute can, by constant practice, readily imagine just such a convenient and comfortable god. They may call him "Jesus" and even write nice little hymns about him, but he is not the Jesus of the Gospels, who certainly would have discouraged any sentimental flying to His bosom and often told men to go out and do most difficult and arduous things. His understanding and sympathy were always at the disposal of those who needed Him, yet the general impression of His personality in the Gospels is of One who was leading men on to fuller understanding and maturity. So far from encouraging them to escape life He came to bring, in His own words, "life more abundant," and in the end He left His followers to carry out a task that might have daunted the stoutest heart. Original Christianity had certainly no taint of escapism.

But those who try to maintain this particular inadequate god today by perpetuating the comfortable protection of early childhood do, probably, unknowingly, a good deal of harm. Here are examples.

1. They prevent themselves from growing up. So long as they imagine that God is saying "Come unto Me" when He is really saying "Go out in My Name," they are preventing themselves from ever putting on spiritual muscle, or developing the right sort of independence—quite apart from the fact that they achieve very little for the cause to which they believe they are devoted.

2. By infecting others with the "to-Thy-bosom-fly" type of piety they may easily encourage those with a tendency that way to remain childish and evade responsibility.

3. By providing the critics with living examples of "escapism" they are responsible for a misrepresentation of the genuine Faith, which repels the psychologically mature who, naturally enough, have no wish to embrace a sentimental Jesus.

4. By "retiring hurt" instead of fighting on, they prevent the implications of the Christian message from touching whole tracts of human life and activity which badly need redeeming. The late Oswald Chambers once asserted that "the Christian has no right to lurk in the bosom of Jesus because his thinking gives

him a headache"—which sums up this aspect of the matter very neatly.

A gibe that was levelled at the early Church was that Christians were nearly all drawn from the criminal or debased slave classes. The answer to the amount of truth contained in that thrust is that those who knew they were sinners, and those who knew how hard life could be, were naturally more likely to respond to a gospel offering a solution to the sinful and oppressed, than those who thought they were "good" and were comfortably protected against many of life's cruelties. But the Christians did not remain criminals after their conversion, and many of the spineless slaves became capable and responsible servants.

Today the gibe is that the message of Christianity attracts only the psychologically immature. Even if that charge were true, the answer to it would be that those who know that they are at sixes and sevens with themselves are more likely to respond to a gospel offering psychological integration (among other things), than those who feel perfectly competent and well-adjusted. Nevertheless the true Christian does not long *remain* either immature or in internal conflict. It is only if he becomes "fixed" with the inadequate god of escape that he exhibits the pathetic figure of the habitual bosom-flyer.

VII. GOD-IN-A-BOX

THE MAN who is outside all organized Christianity
may have, and often does have, a certain reverence
for God, and a certain genuine respect for Jesus
Christ (though he has probably rarely considered
Him and His claims with his adult mind). But what
sticks in his throat about the Christianity of the
Churches is not merely their differences in denomination, but the spirit of "churchiness" which seems to
pervade them all. They seem to him to have captured
and tamed and trained to their own liking Something
that is really far too big ever to be forced into little
man-made boxes with neat labels upon them. He may
never think of putting it into words, but this is what
he thinks and feels.

"If," the Churches appear to be saying to him, "you
will jump through our particular hoop or sign on our
particular dotted line then we will introduce you to
God. But if not, then there's no God for you." This
seems to him to be nonsense, and nasty arrogant nonsense at that. "If there's a God at all," he feels rather
angrily, "then He's here in the home and in the
street, here in the pub and in the workshop. And if
it's true that He's interested in me and wants me to
love and serve Him, then He's available for me and
every other Tom, Dick, or Harry, who wants Him,
without any interference from the professionals. If
God is God, He's *big*, and generous and magnificent,

and I can't see that anybody can say they've made a 'corner' in God, or shut Him up in their particular box."

Of course, it is easy to leap to the defence of the Churches, and point out that every cause must be organized if it is to be effective, that every society must have its rules, that Christ Himself founded a Church, and so on. But if the Churches give the outsider the impression that God works almost exclusively through the machinery they have erected and, what is worse, damns all other machinery which does not bear their label, then they cannot be surprised if he finds their version of God cramped and inadequate and refuses to "join their union."

There are doubtless many reasons for the degeneration of Christianity into churchiness, and the narrowing of the Gospel for all mankind into a set of approved beliefs; but the chief cause must be the worship of an inadequate god, a cramped and regulated god who is "a good churchman" according to the formulas of the worshipper. For actual behaviour infallibly betrays the real object of a man's worship.

All Christians, whatever their Church, would of course instantly repudiate the idea that their god was a super-example of their own denomination, and it is not suggested that the worship is conscious. Nevertheless, beneath the conscious critical level of the mind it is perfectly possible for the Anglo-Catholic, for example, to conceive God as particularly pleased

with Anglo-Catholicism, doubtful about Evangelical-
ism, and frankly displeased by all forms of Noncon-
formity. The Roman Catholic who asserts positively
that ordination in the Anglican Church is "invalid,"
and that no "grace" is receivable through the Anglican sacraments, is plainly worshipping a god who is
a Roman Catholic, and who operates reluctantly, if
at all, through non-Roman channels. The ultra-low
Churchman on the other hand must admit, if he is
honest, that the god whom he worships disapproves
most strongly of vestments, incense, and candles on
the altar. The tragedy of these examples, which could
be reproduced *ad nauseam* any day of the week, is
not difference of opinion, which will probably be
with us till the Day of Judgement, but the outrageous
folly and damnable sin of trying to regard God as the
Party Leader of a particular point of view.

The thoughtful man outside the Churches is not
offended so much by the *differences* of denominations. To him, in his happy ignorance, these are
merely the normal psychological variations of human
taste and temperament being expressed in the religious sphere. What he cannot stomach is the exclusive
claim made by each to be the "right one." His judgement is rightly empirical—did not Christ say, "By
their fruits ye shall know them"? If he were to observe that the Church which makes the boldest and
most exclusive claim to be constituted and maintained
according to Almighty God's own ideas was obviously

producing the finest Christian character, obviously wielding the highest Christian influence, and obviously most filled by the living Spirit of God—he could perhaps forgive the exclusive claim. *But he finds nothing of the kind.* No denomination has a monopoly of God's grace, and none has an exclusive recipe for producing Christian character. It is quite plain to the disinterested observer that the real God takes no notice whatever of the boxes; "the Spirit bloweth where it listeth" and is subject to no regulation of man.

Moreover, our thoughtful observer who is outside the Churches has done a good deal of thinking on his own. The discoveries of modern physical and biological science, of astronomy, and of psychology, have profoundly influenced his conception of the "size" of God. If there be a Mind behind the immense complexities of the phenomena that man can observe, then it is that of a Being tremendous in His power and wisdom: it is emphatically not that of a little god. It is perfectly conceivable that such a Being has a moral purpose which is being worked out on the stage of this small planet. It is even possible to believe that such a God deliberately reduced Himself to the stature of humanity in order to visit the earth in Person, as all Christians affirm. But the sort of thing which outrages reason and sets sanity rocking on her seat is to be told that such a God can only operate where there is an unbroken succession of bishops!

The "outsider" who knows nothing of the mixture of tradition, conviction, honest difference, and hidden resentment, that lies behind the divisions of the Christian Churches sees clearly the advantage of a united Christian front and cannot see why the Churches cannot "get together." The problem is doubtless complicated, for there are many honest differences held with equal sincerity, but it is only made *insoluble* because the different denominations are (possibly unconsciously) imagining God to be Roman Anglican or Baptist or Methodist or Presbyterian or what have you. If they could see beyond their little inadequate god, and glimpse the reality of God, they might even laugh a little and perhaps weep a little. The result would be a unity that actually does transcend differences, instead of ignoring them with public politeness and private contempt.

VIII. MANAGING DIRECTOR

THERE IS a conception of God which seems at first sight to be very lofty and splendid, but which proves paradoxically enough on examination to be yet another of the "too small" ideas. It is to think that the God who is responsible for the terrifying vastnesses of the universe cannot possibly be interested in the lives of the minute specks of consciousness which exist on this insignificant planet.

To have even the beginnings of an appreciation of the greatness of the Power controlling the incredible

System that science is beginning to reveal to us is a staggering but salutary experience. We may feel, since God is so huge and our whole sphere of life (let alone an individual man) is so minute by comparison, that we cannot conceive His taking the detailed interest in a single human life that the protagonists of the Christian religion affirm. To those, and they are not a few, who are secretly wishing for release from moral responsibility (and whose every argument about religion is coloured by the desire), this may be a great relief—the sort of relief that a schoolboy might find in realizing that in a school of a thousand boys his peccadilloes are very unlikely to be noticed by the Headmaster. To others the thought of their insignificance may be desolating—they feel not so much set free as cast adrift.

But whatever a man's reaction may be to the idea of the terrific "size" of God, the point to note is that his comment is this: *"I cannot imagine* such a tremendous God being interested in me," and so on. He "cannot imagine": which means simply that his mind is incapable of retaining the ideas of terrifying vastness and of minute attention to microscopic detail at the same time. But it in no way proves that God is incapable of fulfilling both ideas (and a great many more).

Behind this inability to conceive such a God there probably lies the old unconscious, but very common, cause of "inadequate gods"—the tendency to build up a mental picture of God from our knowledge and experience of man. We know, for instance, that if a man is in charge of fifty other men he can fairly easily make himself familiar with the history, character, abilities, and peculiarities, of each man. If he is in charge of five hundred he may still take a personal interest in each one; but it is almost impossible for him to know and retain in his memory personal details of the individual. If he is in charge of five thousand men he may in general be wise and benevolent; but he cannot, indeed he does not attempt to, know his men as individuals. The higher he is, the fewer his individual contacts. Because in our modern world we are tending more and more to see men amassed in large numbers, for various purposes, we are forced to realize that the individual care of the "one in charge" must grow less and less. This realization has permeated our unconscious minds, and we find it almost inevitably suggested to us that the Highest of All must have the fewest contacts with the individual. Indeed if He is Infinitely High the idea of contact with an infinitesimal individual becomes laughable.

But only if we are modelling God upon what we know of man. That is why it is contended here that what at first sight appears to be almost a super-adequate idea of God is, in reality, inadequate—it is based on too tiny a foundation. Man may be made in the image of God; but it is not sufficient to conceive God as nothing more than an infinitely magnified man.

There are, for example, those who are considerably worried by the thought of God simultaneously hearing and answering the prayers and aspirations of people all over the world. That may be because their mental picture is of a harassed telephone operator answering callers at a switchboard of superhuman size. It is really better to say frankly, "I can't imagine how it can be done" (which is the literal truth), than to confuse the mind with the picture of an enlarged man performing the impossible.

All "lofty" concepts of the greatness of God need to be carefully watched lest they turn out to be mere magnifications of certain human characteristics. We may, for instance, admire the ascetic ultra-spiritual type which appears to have "a mind above" food, sexual attraction, and material comfort, for example. But if in forming a picture of the Holiness of God we are simply enlarging this spirituality and asceticism to the "nth" degree we are forced to some peculiar conclusions. Thus we may find ourselves readily able to imagine God's interest in babies (for are they not "little bits of Heaven"?), yet unable to imagine His approval, let alone design, of the acts which led to their conception!

Similarly it is natural and right, of course, that the worship we offer to God in public should be of the highest possible quality. But that must not lead us to conceive a musically "Third-Programme" god who prefers the exquisite rendering of a cynical professional choir to the ragged bawling of sincere but untutored hearts.

To hold a conception of God as a mere magnified human being is to run the risk of thinking of Him as simply the Commander-in-Chief who cannot possibly spare the time to attend to the details of His subordinates' lives. Yet to have a god who is so far beyond personality and so far removed from the human context in which we alone can appreciate "values," is to have a god who is a mere bunch of perfect qualities—which means an Idea and nothing more. We need a God with the capacity to hold, so to speak, both Big and Small in His Mind at the same time. This, the Christian religion holds, is the true and satisfying conception of God revealed by Jesus Christ, and we will study it further in a later chapter.

IX. SECOND-HAND GOD

MOST PEOPLE, naturally, have a somewhat restricted view of life, and they rely to a far larger extent than they realize on the vicarious experience of life to be found in books, films, and plays. Few of us, for example, have known at all intimately a detective, a dress-designer, a circus-proprietor, a pugilist, or a Harley Street specialist. Yet a skilful writer can make us feel that we have entered the very hearts and lives of these, and many other, people. Almost without question we add what we have read or seen to the

sum total of what we call our "experience." The
process is almost entirely automatic, and probably
most of us would be greatly shocked if it could suddenly be revealed to us how small a proportion of
our accumulated "knowledge of the world" is due to
first-hand observation and experience.

The significance of this second-hand knowledge of
life to the subject we are considering is this: the conception of the Character of God which slowly forms
in our minds is largely made by the conclusions we
draw from the "providences" and "judgements" of
life. We envisage "God" very largely from the way
in which He appears to deal with (or not to deal with)
His creatures. If, therefore, our knowledge of life is
(unknown to us in all probability) faulty or biased
or sentimental, we are quite likely to find ourselves
with a second-hand god who is quite different from
the real one.

There are three main ways in which fiction (in
which term we include books, films, and plays) can
mislead us, and in consequence profoundly affect the
idea we unconsciously hold of God and His operation
in human life.

1. *The tacit ignoring of God and all "religious"
   issues*

A vast amount of fiction presents life as though there
were no God at all, and men and women had no
religious side to their personalities whatever. We may

for instance meet, in fiction, charming people who exhibit the most delightful qualities, surmount incredible difficulties with heart-stirring courage, make the most noble sacrifices and achieve the utmost happiness and serenity—all without the slightest reference to God. The reader is almost bound to reflect that all the fuss Christianity makes about "seeking God's strength" and so on is much ado about nothing.

Conversely, we not infrequently read of evil characters who, for all their lust, cruelty, meanness, or pride, never seem to suffer the faintest twinge of conscience. There appears to be no spiritual force at work pointing out to them, at vulnerable moments, a better way of living; and repentance is unthinkable. The reader is again, unconsciously, likely to conclude that God does nothing to influence "bad" characters.

This by-pass which neatly avoids God and the religious side of life is not characteristic perhaps of the very best fiction, but it is extremely common. In films in particular, with a few notable exceptions, "providence" is subject to almost cast-iron conventions. These include the socially desirable "crime-does-not-pay" ethic, and the inevitable happy ending. But any resemblance between the celluloid providence and the real actions of God in human affairs is purely coincidental.

In actual life, as any parson worth his salt well knows, ordinary people do at times consider God and spiritual issues. The evil, and even the careless, are occasionally touched by their consciences. Moreover, the tensions and crises which are the breath of life to the fiction-writer are the very things which frequently stimulate the latent spiritual or religious sense. It is an extraordinary phenomenon that the modern writer who has, Heaven knows, few reticences and who is sometimes almost morbidly analytical of his characters' actions, should so frequently use the by-pass road round the whole sphere of a man's relations with his God.

2. *The wilful misrepresentation of religion*

It can of course be argued that it is no part of the duty of a writer of fiction to provide Christian propaganda—and that is perfectly true. But it is equally no part of his work, which is "to hold up a mirror to life," to give the impression that Christianity and the Church are no more than a subject for ridicule. It may of course be great fun for him—he may be working off a childhood grudge against an Evangelical aunt—to represent clergymen as comic, bigoted, or childishly ignorant of life, and Christians as smug hypocrites. He may even feel that there is more dramatic value in the rector who is a domestic tyrant or the nonconformist deacon who is a secret sadist than in the genuine articles. But he is not, in so doing, being fair to the actual facts of life, even though his writing may prove highly gratifying to the reader who is only too ready to welcome this endorsement of his own feeling that "religion is all rot anyway."

Again, this criticism cannot fairly be levelled at the best fiction, but it is extremely common in the popular type, and slowly but surely affects the conception of religion and of God in the minds of many readers.

3. *The manipulation of providence*

The author of fiction (and this is not the least of the attractions of authorship) is in the position of a god to his own creatures. He can move in a mysterious way, or an outrageous way, or an unjust way, his wonders to perform; and no one can say him nay. If he works skilfully (as, for instance, did Thomas Hardy) he may strongly infect his reader with, for example, the sense of a bitterly jesting Fate in place of God. He can communicate heartbreak by the simplest of manipulations, because he is himself providence, *but he is not thereby providing any evidence of the workings of real life.*

The whole tragedy of King Lear might be said to depend on Shakespeare's manipulation of the character of Cordelia. Because she is unable to see (though every schoolgirl in the pit can see) the probable consequence of her blunt "Nothing" the tragedy is launched. But it would be a profound mistake to confuse the organized disasters of even the greatest writer of tragedy with the complex circumstances and factors which attend the sufferings of real life.

Conclusions as to the nature of Life and God can only in very rare instances be inferred from the artificial evidence of fiction. We need therefore to be constantly on our guard against the "Second-hand god"—the kind of god which the continual absorption of fictional ideas nourishes at the back of our minds. One tiny slice of real life, observed at first hand, provides better grounds for our conclusions than the whole fairy world of fiction.

X. PERENNIAL GRIEVANCE

To some people the mental image of God is a kind of blur of disappointment. "Here," they say resentfully and usually with more than a trace of self-pity, "is One whom I trusted, but He *let me down*." The rest of their lives is consequently shadowed by this letdown. Thenceforth there can be no mention of God, Church, religion, or even parson, without starting the whole process of association with its melancholy conclusion: God is a Disappointment.

Some, of course, rather enjoy this never-failing well of grievance. The years by no means dim the tragic details of the Prayer that was Unanswered or the Disaster that was Undeserved. To recall God's unfaithfulness appears to give them the same ghoulish pleasure that others find in recounting the grisly details of their "operation." Others find, of course, that a God who has Himself failed is the best possible excuse for those who do not wish to be involved in any moral effort or moral responsibility. Any suggestion of obeying or following God can be more than countered by another glance at the perennial Grievance.

Such a god is, of course, in the highest degree inadequate. It is impossible for people who have persuaded themselves that God has failed, to worship or serve Him in any but a grudging and perfunctory spirit. What has usually happened to such people is that they have set up in their minds what they think God ought or ought not to do, and when He apparently fails to toe their particular line they feel a sense of grievance. Yet it is surely more sensible, as well as more fitting, for us human beings to find out, as far as we can, the ways in which God works. We have to discover as far as we can the limits He has set Himself for the purposes of this Great Experiment that we call Life—and then do our best to align ourselves with the principles and co-operate with the purposes that we have certainly had no say in deciding, but which nevertheless in our highest moments we know are good. God will inevitably appear to disappoint the man who is attempting to use Him as a convenience, a prop, or a comfort, for his own plans. God has never been known to disappoint the man who is sincerely wanting to co-operate with His own purposes.

It must be freely admitted that, in this experimental world, to which God has given the risky privilege of free-will, there are inevitably "ills and accidents." Moreover, the cumulative effect over the centuries of millions of individuals' choosing to please themselves rather than the Designer of "the whole show" has infected the whole planet. That is what the theologians mean when they call this a "sinful" world. This naturally means that, so far as this world is concerned, the tough, insensitive, and selfish, will frequently appear to get away with it, while the weak and sensitive will often suffer. Once we admit the possibilities of free-will we can see that injustices and grievances are inevitable. (As Christ once said: "It must needs be that offences come.") We may not agree with the risk that God took in giving Man the power to choose—we might even have preferred God to make a race of robots who were unfailingly good and cheerful and kind. But it is not in the least a question of what God *could have done,* but a question of what *He has done.* We have to accept the Scheme of Things as it is, and if we must blame someone it is surely fairer to blame Man who has chosen wrongly and produced a world awry.

The people who feel that God is a Disappointment have not understood the terms on which we inhabit this planet. They are wanting a world in which good is rewarded and evil is punished—as in a well-run kindergarten. They want to see the good man prosper invariably, and the evil man suffer invariably, here and now. There is, of course, nothing wrong with their sense of justice. But they misunderstand the conditions of this present temporary life in which God withholds His Hand, in order, so to speak, to allow room for His plan of free-will to work itself out. Justice will be fully vindicated when the curtain falls on the present stage, the house-lights go on, and we go out into the Real World.

There will always be times when from our present limited point of view we cannot see the wood for the trees. Glaring injustice and pointless tragedy will sometimes be quite beyond our control and our understanding. We can, of course, postulate an imaginary God with less good sense, love and justice than we have ourselves, and we may find a perverse pleasure in blaming him. But that road leads nowhere. You cannot worship a Disappointment.

XI. PALE GALILEAN

IF THEY were completely honest, many people would have to admit that God is to them an almost entirely negative force in their lives. It is not merely that He provides that "gentle voice we hear . . . which checks each fault," but that His whole Nature seems to deny, to cramp, and inhibit their own. Though such people would never admit it, they are living endorsements of Swinburne's bitter lines:

Thou hast conquered, O pale Galilean,
The world has grown grey from Thy breath.

Compared with their non-Christian contemporaries their lives seem to have less life and colour, less spontaneity and less confidence. Their god surrounds them with prohibitions but he does not supply them with vitality and courage. They may live under the shadow of his hand but it makes them stunted, pale and weak. Although the thought would appear blasphemous to his devotees, such a god is quite literally a blight upon human life, and no one can be surprised that he fails to attract the loyalty of those with spirit, independence, and a keen enjoyment of the colour and richness of life.

The words written above are a plain exposure of a false god, but of course the unhappy worshippers never see their bondage as clearly as that or they would break away. They are bound to their negative god by upbringing, by the traditions of a Church or party, by the manipulation of isolated texts of Scripture or by a morbid conscience. At last they actually feel that it is wrong to be themselves, wrong to be free, wrong to enjoy beauty, wrong to expand and develop. Unless they have their god's permission they can do nothing. Disaster will infallibly bring them to heel, sooner or later, should they venture beyond the confines of "his plan for them."

Such people, naturally enough, can only by strenuous efforts maintain their narrow loyalty. They do not get the chance to admire and love and worship in wordless longing One who is overwhelmingly splendid and beautiful and lovable. At best they can only love and worship because their god is a jealous god, and it is his will and commandment that they should. Their lives are cramped and narrow and joyless, because their god is the same.

There must be compensations in the worship of such a god, and they are usually these.

1. The belief that the joy and freedom of those who do *not* subscribe to the worship of the negative god is just an illusion. Negative god worshippers often sustain themselves by imagining and elaborating upon the inner strains and conflicts of those who do not know their god. In fact, the strains and conflicts of ordinary life are quite rightly felt by sensible people to be preferable to the intolerable and neverending strain of worshipping a god who drains life of all its vitality and colour.

2. There is a certain spiritually masochistic joy in being crushed by the juggernaut of a negative god. This is perfectly brought out in a hymn which is still sung in certain circles:

> Oh to be nothing, nothing,
> Only to lie at His feet,
> A broken and emptied vessel
> For the Master's use made meet.

The sense of humour is, of course, suspended by the negative god, or his devotees would be bound to see the absurdity of anyone's ambition being to be "nothing," a "broken" and, not unnaturally, "emptied" vessel lying at God's feet! Better still, the New Testament (a book full of freedom and joy, courage and vitality) might be searched in vain to supply any endorsement whatsoever of the above truly dreadful verse and the conception of God it typifies. If ever a book taught men to be "something, something," to stand and do battle, to be far more full of joy and daring and life than they ever were without God—that book is the New Testament!

3.   The comforting idea of being "something special." Worshippers of the negative god often comfort themselves by feeling that what is good enough for "the world" is not good enough for them: the chosen, the unique. Even though this means a life denuded of the beauties of art, of normal pleasures and recreation, a life cramped in all normal means of expression —that is a small price to pay for being the separate, the unique.

This pathetic idea of being "something special" is clung to with desperation, so that we find worshippers of the negative god who know in their secret hearts that their lives cannot really exhibit any superior qualities to those of their "worldly" or "worldly Christian" friends, clinging tightly to their rules of "separateness"—so that they may at least feel that they are marked out as the especial favourites of their god!

All this is very unattractive and unpleasant, but it

is quite common among religious people. The question for them is: dare they defy and break away from this imaginary god with the perpetual frown and find the One who is the great Positive, who gives life, courage and joy, and wants His sons and daughters to stand on their own feet?

XII. PROJECTED IMAGE

JUST AS the cinema apparatus projects on to the screen a large image from a picture about the size of a postage stamp, so the human mind has a tendency to "project" on to other people ideas and emotions that really exist in itself. The guilty man, for example, will project on to other people suspicion and disapproval, even though they are completely ignorant of his guilt. This, of course, is an everyday psychological phenomenon.

We tend to do the same thing in our mental conception of God. (As has already been pointed out there are some who would go so far as to say the whole idea of God is simply a "projection" in adult life of the childish desire for a Father's protection; but this we cannot accept for the reasons given above.) A harsh and puritanical society will project its dominant qualities and probably postulate a hard and puritanical god. A lax and easy-going society will probably produce a god with about as much moral authority as Father Christmas.

The same tendency is observable in individual
cases. We have already noted in "God-in-a-box" how
a certain type of keen churchman, for example, tends
to produce a god of Impeccable Churchmanship. But,
of course, the inclination goes farther than this, and
there is always a danger of imagining a god with
moral qualities like our own, vastly magnified and
purified of course, and *with the same blind spots.*
Thus the god whom we imagine may have his face
set against drunkenness (an evil which, though it
does not tempt us, fills us with horror and indigna-
tion), may turn a blind eye to our business methods
because he feels, as we do, that "business is business"!

Obviously, unless the conception of God is something higher than a Magnification of our own Good
Qualities, our service and worship will be no more
and no less than the service and worship of ourselves.
Such a god may be a prop to our self-esteem but is,
naturally, incapable of assisting us to win a moral
victory and will be found in time of serious need to
fade disconcertingly away.

Moreover, we are so made that we cannot really
be satisfied with a mere projection. Even Narcissus
must at times have grown tired of admiring his own
reflection! The very fact that in choosing a friend or
a life-partner men frequently choose someone very
different from themselves is enough to show that they
are not only and for ever seeking an echo of their
own personalities. If we are to be moved to real wor-

ship and stirred to give ourselves, it must be by Something not merely infinitely higher but Something "other" than ourselves.

The Christian answer to this need we shall consider later on, and we will do no more than point out here that the god who is wholly, or even partially, a mere projection of ourselves is quite inadequate for life's demands and can never arouse in us true worship or service. Indeed he is as real a danger as the pool became at last to Narcissus.

XIII. ASSORTED

THE FOREGOING round dozen do not by any means exhaust the little gods which infest human minds. Too much space would be occupied by fully describing them all, but a brief description of a few more may suffice to expose their falsity.

God in a hurry

If there is one thing which should be quite plain to those who accept the revelation of God in Nature and the Bible it is that He is never in a hurry. Long preparation, careful planning, and slow growth, would seem to be leading characteristics of spiritual life. Yet there are many people whose religious tempo is feverish. With a fine disregard for its context they flourish like a banner the text, "The King's business requireth haste," and proceed to drive themselves and

their followers nearly mad with tension and anxiety!
"Consider," cries the passionate advocate of foreign
missions, "that every second, thousands of pagan souls
pass into a Christless eternity." "Evangelize to a finish
in this generation!" cries the enthusiastic young con-
vert at his missionary meeting.

It is refreshing, and salutary, to study the poise and
quietness of Christ. His task and responsibility might
well have driven a man out of his mind. But he was
never in a hurry, never impressed by numbers, never
a slave of the clock. He was acting, he said, as he
observed God to act—never in a hurry.

God for the Elite

It is characteristic of human beings to create and
revere a "privileged class," and some modern Christians regard the mystic as being somehow spiritually
a cut above his fellows. Ordinary forms of worship
and prayer may suffice for the ordinary man, but for
the one who has direct apprehension of God—he is
literally in a class by himself. You cannot expect a
man to attend Evensong in his parish church when
there are visions waiting for him in his study!

The New Testament does not subscribe to this
flattering view of those with a gift for mystic vision.
It is always downright and practical. It is by their
fruits that men shall be known: God is no respecter
of persons: true religion is expressed by such hum-
drum things as visiting those in trouble and stead-

fastly maintaining faith despite exterior circumstances. It is not, of course, that the New Testament considers it a bad thing for a man to have a vision of God, but there is a wholesome insistence on such a vision being worked out in love and service.

It should be noted, at least by those who accept Christ's claim to be God, that he by no means fits into the picture of the "mystic saint." Those who are fascinated by the supposed superiority of the mystic soul might profitably compile a list of its characteristics and place them side by side with those of Christ. The result would probably expose a surprising conclusion.

There is, in fact, no provision for a "privileged class" in genuine Christianity. "It shall not be so among you," said Christ to his early followers, "all ye are brethren."

God of Bethel

There are quite a number of religious people who might fairly be said, if the truth were told, to be more at home with Jehovah than with Jesus Christ. The Old Testament, again if the truth were told, means more to them than the New.

These are the people who see religion as a contract: they obey certain rules and God will faithfully look after them and their interests. These are the people who write to the papers and say "if only" the nation would obey the Ten Commandments then God would grant victory, or rain, or fine weather, or whatever the need of the moment may be. They like everything cut-and-dried and even the Gospel is reduced to a formula; so that if you sign on the dotted line, so to speak, you are all right for heaven! They prefer the letter to the spirit and definite commandments to vague principles. They more usually refer to "the Lord" than to "God."

Such people have not appreciated the revolutionary character of God's invasion of the world in Christ, though they would be horrified if it were suggested that they have not yet accepted the import of his pronouncement: "It hath been said of old time . . . *but I say unto you.*"

But their Old Testament God will not suffice for the hunger of modern man, however they may wring their hands at the "unbelief" of today. God is not a God of the dead, but of the living.

God without Godhead

This conception is one of the most "enlightened" and "modern." God is completely de-personalized and becomes the Ultimate Bundle of Highest Values. Such an idea is usually held by those who lead sheltered lives and who have little experience of the crude stuff of ordinary human life. It is manifestly impossible for any except the most intellectual to hold in his mind (let alone worship and serve) a God

who is no more than what we think to be the highest
values raised to the nth degree.

Gods by any other Name

Man has rightly been defined as a "worshipping
animal." If for some reason he has no God he will
unquestionably worship *something*. Common modern substitutes are the following: the State, success,
efficiency, money, "glamour," power, even security.
Nobody, of course, calls them "God"; but they have
the influence and command the devotion which
should belong to the real God. It is only when a man
finds God that he is able to see how his worshipping
instinct has been distorted and mis-directed.

TRANSITIONAL NOTE

Before proceeding to the second part of this work the
author feels that a short word of explanation is due.

It is not our intention to build up merely a bigger
and better god, who may be just as much an artificial-
ity as any of the unattractive galaxy we have dis-
carded. What we are going to try to do is to open the
windows of the mind and spirit—to put it crudely,
to enlarge the aperture through which the light of
the true God may shine. If a man lives in a light-
proof room the sun may shine in dazzling splendour
and the man himself will know nothing of it. He may

light himself a candle or he may bore a hole in his prison. In the first case he can never have more than an artificial glimmer, and in the second he will get only a tiny glimpse of real daylight. Some of the gods we have considered are nothing more than artificial; some of them are inadequate pin-hole glimpses of the true Light. What we are going to try to do, then, is not to light fresh candles but to take down the shutters. There is no reason why we should be content with the candle or the pin-hole if a little determined thinking and a little sincere action will remove the shutters.

AN ADEQUATE GOD

I. GOD UNFOCUSED

IT MAY SEEM to some that a great deal of time has been spent in "clearing the ground": but it is absolutely necessary. We shall never want to serve God in our real and secret hearts if He looms in our subconscious mind as an arbitrary Dictator or a Spoilsport, or as one who takes advantage of His position to make us poor mortals feel guilty and afraid. We have not only to be impressed by the "size" and unlimited power of God, we have to be moved to genuine admiration, respect, and affection, if we are ever to worship Him.

First, however, let us fling wide the doors and windows of our minds and make some attempt to appreciate the "size" of God. He must not be limited to religious matters or even to the "religious" interpretation of life. He must not be confined to one particular section of time nor must we imagine Him as the local god of this planet or even only of the universe that astronomical survey has so far discovered. It is not, of course, physical size that we are trying to establish in our minds. (Physical size is not important. By any reasonable scheme of values a human being is of vastly greater worth than a mountain ten million times his physical size.) It is rather to see the immensely broad sweep of the Creator's activity, the astonishing complexity of His mental processes which science laboriously uncovers, the vast sea of what we can only call "God" in a small corner of which man lives and moves and has his being.

To meditate on this broadness and vastness will do much to expose the inadequate little gods, but if we stop there we may get no farther than sensing a vague "unfocused" God, a de-personalized "Something" which is after a while peculiarly unsatisfying.

There are those who would make this "Something" the God of the future. Building up a mental concept from known values like Goodness, Truth, and Beauty, they would have us hold in our minds and worship in our hearts the Source of Supreme Values. Such a God is not a Person in any sense, and though such an idea seems to satisfy some of the most intellectual of our time it does not, and probably will never, satisfy the ordinary man. It certainly does not appear to supply a Gospel to redeem the despairs and futilities of life, nor does it in practice appear to provide a spear-head against old-established evils. To worship, to love, and to serve, implies for most of us a Person with whom we can establish some personal relationship, although one cannot help pointing out that one great attraction of a non-personal God is that no claim can be made upon us! He (or It) may be used as much or as little as we like!

Thus we can see the dilemma, though often unconscious, of many modern people outside organized religion. If they use their minds and imaginations they cannot help seeing that if there is a Supreme Being He must be infinitely vaster than our forefathers' conceptions. The more they know, the more science reveals to them, the wider grow the mental horizons and the more inadequate grow the old little gods. And yet this vastness seems to de-personalize God more and more until he becomes a vague unfocused Abstraction.

In the face of this dilemma many abandon the idea of knowing God, and pin their hopes and apply their energies to the "progress" of the human race. In despair at ever coming to terms with "eternal" values, they get a certain amount of satisfaction in improving the "here and now," concerning themselves with present values of which they are reasonably sure.

Yet, in fact, unless we can relate this activity to God, i.e. to Something beyond time and space, it is a singularly fatuous thing to do, and we only need a few logical steps to appreciate it. Let us admit for the moment that we *are* making progress, that the human race for all its devastating wars is becoming slowly and surely more and more healthy, wealthy and wise. Suppose that this process, notwithstanding set-backs, continues for thousands, even millions of years. Presumably, then, at some time in the very remote future the human beings then living on this planet will have conquered Nature by scientific knowledge, will have resolved all tensions and maladjustments of personal relationships by vastly improved psychological methods, and will be living lives of almost unbelievable health and happiness and satisfaction. That, we may fairly say, is the aim of those who freely give their energies to the progress of the human race, and who exhort us to "live for posterity." But what then? This planet eventually, as far as our knowledge goes, either will become too cold to support life (even by artificial means), or will be destroyed by collision with some other heavenly body. That means that the total result of human progress, of every effort and aspiration and ideal will be annihilation in the deathly cold of inter-stellar space. And there is nothing more to come.

Yet this—human progress—is to many the greatest value for which to live. Of course if they stop short of the final scene they may persuade themselves that the eventual happiness of our descendants a million years hence is a worthy ideal for which to live and die. But if the end is *nothing, sheer non-existence,* surely no reasonable person can regard it as an ideal to command the whole loyalty of an adult mind and heart.

II. A CLUE TO REALITY

THE DISCOVERY of the enormous energy released by nuclear fission and the unforgettable demonstrations of the destructive power of the "atom bomb" have done us a service in our quest for Reality that perhaps we hardly realize. They have demonstrated before the whole world that what we call "matter" is in fact destructible. Those things that we formerly regarded as almost imperishable, such as armour-plate and concrete, could, under certain conditions, be dissipated into vapour less substantial than the smoke from a cigarette. Indeed, since the whole stuff of our planet, animate and inanimate, is composed of variously arranged atoms, it is by no means unthinkable that some experiment or deliberate act might result in a chain-reaction, exploding, so to speak, every atom of which this world is composed. Whether we like it or not we live now under the shadow of such universal disintegration. This can hardly do other than set our minds to value far more highly than ever before the "spiritual" values. By these we mean the qualities of spirit, of personality, which are recognizable and assessable, but are incapable either of scientific weighing and measuring

—and incapable of physical destruction. In the light of the probable ultimate fate of the planet and of the present (far more impressive) threat to human life, we are driven to reconsider whether after all there is reality beyond the physical, measurable, reality. We begin to wonder whether the whole position is not now the reverse of what men once thought. They used to talk of the "spiritual" values as shadowy and unsubstantial, and the physical as solid and "real" and reliable. They are beginning to see that the opposite may well be true. We can certainly see evidence of the universal destructibility of matter: perhaps it is after all true that "reality" lies in another realm altogether, and that its values are not unsubstantial after all.

This, of course, is far more readily believed by some temperaments than by others. The poets, artists, and philosophers, as well as a great many other undistinguished people, of many ages, have probably been more or less acutely conscious that the "spiritual" is of vastly greater importance than the material. To all of them, speaking broadly, this present physical life is the visible and tangible stage or battlefield of spiritual forces. Universal values, such as truth, goodness, and beauty, were often considered to exist apart from, as well as being exhibited in, the life of this world. To some of them this present life is merely the prelude, lived under difficulty and handicap, to a free unfettered life of the spirit. The latter is reality

—the former is an important but transitory incident.

This age-long intuition is now being forced upon humanity as a strong and workable hypothesis by the threatened disintegration of the merely physical. And there is enough inward assent to it in the hearts of most men to give them at any rate one powerful clue to reality. It makes the idea of God far more sensible and far more desirable.

After all, if it should be true that the nature of reality is spiritual and it is only quite temporarily and incidentally involved in matter, it is not unreasonable to want to know something of the Spiritual Being behind the Scheme of Things. And on those unimaginative people to whom the spiritual has always sounded fanciful and unreal, it is slowly dawning that the physical world which is so real and tangible to them is most uncomfortably unreliable. A man used to be able to reckon on a good number of years of active material life, which were a most efficient buffer between him and the naked spiritual realities which in his more vulnerable moments he suspected might be true. Now his buffer of material things has been shown to be far from dependable. At any moment he might be pitchforked into the world of the spirit. His anchors are slipping, and if he feels the need of anchorage (and who, at heart, does not?) he must find it in the world of the spirit—he must find God.

NOTE. It must not be supposed that what we call

spiritual (and which is at present invisible) is less "solid" than matter. It may well prove, since it is indestructible, to be in a sense, *more* solid. It is only our peculiar way of looking at things which makes a man's muscles, for example, appear more solid than his "spiritual" assets of personality. This idea of the real world being more "solid" is most ably and ingeniously worked out by Dr. C. S. Lewis in his fantasy of Heaven and Hell: *The Great Divorce*.

III. FURTHER CLUES TO REALITY

IN ALL probability everyone is sensitive to beauty, although obviously some are far more so than others. Yet experience shows that even those who are apparently most prosaic are touched, even to their own surprise, by certain forms of beauty. The line along which this half-melancholy, half-magic touch may come varies enormously with different people. For some it is the appealing grace of childhood, for some the surge and thunder of the sea, for some the dazzling splendour of mountain peak, for some the song of birds in spring, for some the smell of wood-smoke or of frosty autumn evenings, for some—but the list is endless. All poetry and music, and art of every true sort, bears witness to man's continual falling in love with beauty, and his desperate attempt to induce beauty to live with him and enrich his common life.

True beauty always seems to bear with it a note of gentle sadness, sometimes very poignant; and it may well puzzle us why this should be so. If the beautiful is so desirable and so welcome it should surely bring unqualified joy. There is rarely accompanying sadness in other earthly joys. In the enjoyment of a hearty meal, in the successful solving of a difficult problem, or in the fulfilment of creative activity, there is joy, but no melancholy. Is it possible that beauty is a hint of the real and true and permanent, so that we feel without conscious process of thought: "This is what life should be, or what it *is* in reality." And therefore to compare *that* with our ordinary everyday experience with all its imperfection and ugliness gives rise to the poignant pain? Or is it, as some hold, fancifully perhaps, a kind of nostalgia— what Wordsworth would call an "intimation of immortality." Is it the eternal spirit in a man remembering here in his house of clay the shining joys of his real Home?

No one, of course, can say. But the appeal of beauty which is universal, however distorted or debased it may have become, cannot be lightly dismissed. It is a pointer to something, and it certainly points to something beyond the present limitations of time and space. We can at any rate say that beauty arouses a hunger and a longing which is never satisfied (and some would say never can be satisfied) in this world.

The second clue to the nature of reality is what we can only call by the slightly forbidding title of "goodness." Disabusing our minds of self-conscious righteousness, goody-goodyness and mere absence of evil, there is something unavoidably attractive about the good. However far from the ideal our own practice may be, we have an automatic respect for such things as honesty, sincerity, faithfulness, incorruptibility, kindness, justice, and respect for other people. Indeed, we hardly saw the significance of our acknowledgement of the worth of these things until they were directly challenged by the late Nazi régime. Even now a great many people have hardly grasped the significance of the fact that we, in common with millions of others, denounced the treachery, brutality, lies, and cynical denial of traditional moral values, as "evil things." Unless our feeling for goodness is a clue to ultimate Reality the most we can do is to say that we personally dislike the characteristics of the Nazi philosophy. Unless there is some moral standard to which we are (unconsciously) referring the question, it can be no more than mere difference of opinion. The Nazi had a perfect right to say that he disliked our moral values, and who is to say whether he or we were in the right? To reply that methods of treachery, brutality, and inhumanity, offend the universal conscience of mankind is to establish more firmly the point we are trying to make. *Why* is there this almost universal moral sense? Why do we consider that "good" is a better thing than "evil"? Surely this recognition of good, so deeply rooted and so universal, is another far from negligible pointer to Reality.

Both beauty and goodness, then (no doubt in different ways), exert an effect upon man which cannot be explained in terms of the world that we know, and to this we may add his search for truth. He is not only wanting to know facts, though the careful dispassionate amassing of ascertained facts is surely one of his most admirable activities, but he also wants to find some meaning to the puzzle of life. Scientific research, philosophy and religion, all in their different ways attest this reaching out of man to grasp more and more truth. And yet—why should he? Why should he not rest content with what he has and what he knows? Why can he not accept death and evil and disease without worrying about them? Why does he, in all ages and in all countries, reach out to find Something —something which will harmonize and explain and complete life's bewildering phenomena? Here, too, is surely a pointer. Arguing, as we must, from what we know to what we don't know, we may fairly say that as food is the answer to hunger, water the answer to thirst, and a mate to sexual desire, this universal hunger for Truth is unlikely to be without its answer and fulfilment, however hard to find it may be.

IV. IS THERE A FOCUSED GOD?

BEAUTY, Goodness, and Truth, wherever they occur, are certainly clues; but they seem to be like cameras focused "to infinity"—we cannot tell how far and how great is the Reality to which they are pointing.

Now although everyone knows what is meant by Beauty, Goodness, and Truth, it is impossible to visualize them as absolute values. We can visualize a beautiful thing, but not beauty; a good man, but not goodness; a true fact, but not truth. Yet once we have a beautiful thing held in our minds it is comparatively easy to fill the mind with other beauties; once we consider a truly good man we can expand and develop his qualities until we begin to get some idea of goodness; while if we are once convinced of a certain fact (particularly if we have discovered it ourselves), we can at once think of a world of truths— we begin to visualize the absolute quality of Truth.

We see beauty, then, when it is first focused for us in a beautiful thing; goodness when it is focused in a good man; truth when it is focused in a fact of which we are sure. Absolute values may exist as mental concepts for the trained philosopher; but the ordinary man must see his values focused in people or things that he knows before he can grasp them.

Let us now make a further step. The mystic claims to be able to grasp something of God in the Absolute. But the mystic is even more uncommon than the philosopher, and any attempt by the ordinary man to "imagine" God results in nothing but the "vague oblong blur" complained of by those modern people who make the attempt. Yet if a man can see God focused and be convinced that he is seeing God, scaled-down but authentic, he can, as in the case of

Beauty, Truth, and Goodness, add all the other inklings and impressions that he has of the majesty, magnificence, and order of the Infinite Being, and "see God."

But can he so see God "focused"? There must be more than elusive sparks and flashes of the divine—there must be a flame burning steadily so that its light can be examined and properly assessed.

It is a fascinating problem for us human beings to consider how the Eternal Being—wishing to show men His own Character focused, His own Thought expressed, and His own Purpose demonstrated—could introduce Himself into the stream of human history without disturbing or disrupting it. There must obviously be an almost unbelievable "scaling-down" of the "size" of God to match the life of the planet. There must be a complete acceptance of the space-and-time limitations of this present life. The thing must be done properly—it must not, for example, be merely an act put on for man's benefit. If it is to be done at all God must *be* man. There could be no convincing focusing of real God in some strange semi-divine creature who enjoys supernatural advantages. Nor, though it is plain that many men have been "inspired" to utter truth, to create beauty and to demonstrate goodness, could it suffice for a unique and authentic focusing to depend on one "super-inspired" man. For complete dependability, for universal appeal, for a personally guaranteed authenticity to which all other truth is to be related, God must do it Himself.

Suppose, then, that God does slip into the stream of history and is born as Baby *A*. *A* will, as far as the limitations of time, space, and circumstance allow, grow up as God "focused" in humanity, speaking a language, expressing thoughts, and demonstrating life in terms that men can understand. Having once accepted *A*'s claim to be God expressing Himself in human terms, men will have a great deal by which to live.

First, they will know now for certain what sort of "character" the eternal God possesses. For He is certain to inform them that the man who observes Him is observing God. Secondly, the facts about man and God, the perennial anxieties about such things as pain and sin and death, the dim hopes of a more permanent world to follow this one—these and scores of other clamant questions will now have a fixed reference point, by which they can be adjusted if not settled. Thirdly, man will be able to gain at first hand information as to "what life is all about" and as to how he can co-operate with the Plan and the Power behind time and space. Fourthly, if they are convinced, as we are assuming, that the one before them is really God-become-man, they will be able to observe something absolutely unique in the history of the world: God Himself coping with life on the very terms that He has imposed upon His creatures. They will be seeing God not seated high on a throne, but down in the battlefield of life.

A, of course, having genuinely entered the space-time world and having become a human being, must enter at some particular time and must live in some particular locality. He will thus, as far as some incidentals and externals are concerned, be to some extent moulded, modified, and limited. He cannot, therefore, be a *full* expression of God—there is neither time nor space enough for that. But within the limit he sets himself he will be a perfectly genuine and adequate focusing of the nature of God. He will not only be information and example, but the aperture through which men may see more and more of God. If men are once convinced of the genuineness of his extraordinary claim, they will probably find that God is, so to speak, visible through an *A*-shaped aperture. Knowledge, experience, and appreciation, may all expand enormously as the years pass, but that will not mean that men "grow out of" God. For *A* will have supplied by his demonstration in time and space one sure Fact, around which everything else of Truth, Goodness, and Beauty, may be appropriately and satisfactorily crystallized.

V. IF GOD WERE FOCUSED (I)

If *A*, THEN, does enter the life of this planet there will be certain phenomena which would appear to be inevitable, unless (on a possibility we are not considering) the normal rules of life are temporarily suspended.

In the first place it is unlikely that *A* will be recognized as God in any real sense, at any rate for some time. Men would almost certainly judge any alleged personal appearance of God in life by two criteria. First, they would probably expect some definitely numinous quality to be invariably present. They would expect to feel frightened or to see an aura of divinity, or witness supernormal powers. In other words, they would not expect God *really* to be man, but only to be pretending to be one—and that is not the same thing at all. God pretending to be man could, for example, achieve all kinds of superhuman feats in the moral, mental, spiritual, or even physical realm. That might impress, but it would leave a man where he was before; he would be no nearer *understanding* or knowing God. He might be dazzled, but he would remain unilluminated. Secondly, men would almost certainly, if the first possibility did not occur, expect to see a "holy-man" of the super-mystic type, someone whose wisdom is too profound for words and whose eyes are too intent upon heavenly realities to be *au fait* with the commonplace world. If *A* then is revealed as a perfectly adjusted, wholesome, sane, and non-fanatical man, his claim to be God (which he must make in due course, unless someone suddenly grasps the truth) will be looked upon as fantastic and blasphemous. If *A* makes his appearance among those who have so exalted their conception of God that for Him ever to wear the soiled robe of sinful humanity is an unthinkable degradation of his Godhead, the task for *A* will be immeasurably harder. But if he appears among those who have always thought that there was some hint of God in the character of man, then some at least may well see what is happening. It would be those who depreciate or even despise humanity in order to exalt their idea of God who would in all probability be completely blind to *A*'s identity.

Yet there will be, naturally, something about *A* in addition to a well-balanced and wholesome personality. There will, for instance, be a certain tone of authority—the quiet assurance of the expert speaking on his own subject—when he speaks of the basic facts of life, of man, and of God. Unless their inklings and intuitions are all wrong, men will find, probably not without emotion, that in *A*'s teaching is the quiet logical assembly of all the isolated flashes of insight that they have ever experienced. "What this man is saying," some of them at least are bound to feel, "is true. This is reality. This is what we have always hoped God would be like, and this is what we have always felt that life should be like." For unless this is a completely insane world or a hopelessly evil one, *A*'s words must strike an answering chord in the hearts of many ordinary people.

It will not of course be only A's words that tell. If he is to enjoy no supernatural advantages, he will get his share of trouble and temptation, trial and disappointment, and his reactions to these, as well as to every other part of life, pleasant or unpleasant, will produce a certain definite impression. He will be revealing a character. Whether his friends and observers realize it at the time or not, he will be showing them not only the character of the Invisible God focused and functioning in ordinary human circumstances, but an example of perfect humanity. What actually happens to him will of course depend on when and where God decides on this insertion of Himself into history, but in a sense it would always be the same, for the Character expressed in human terms will be the same and the Example will always follow the same pattern. This is an important point, for it makes the demonstration, provided that there is an accurate record of it available, of universal value. The personal invasion need not be continually repeated.

We may reasonably surmise, that the world being what it is, there will be other reactions than the glad recognition of A's teaching as true. For in practice men do not by any means always "love the highest when they see it," and truth is not always a welcome visitor. We could probably therefore credibly forecast a good deal of opposition and misrepresentation. These things we should certainly look for in A's visit:

1. A challenge to current moral values, and possibly even some downright reversals of conventional judgement. The love of money or position, the lust for success, and the desire to keep all unpleasant matters safely out of sight, warp the world's judgement probably more than it knows. *A*'s values are therefore likely to be found more than a trifle disconcerting, though probably they will be dismissed as "fine ideals but wholly impracticable."

2. A disturbing probing into motive rather than measurable performance. *A*, seeing life from the true instead of the conventional point of view, will seem to have disconcerting insight into what is normally concealed. This will make him enemies as well as friends.

3. An insistence on real human values, and particularly on love of the right kind. *A* will naturally see through the glamours and clevernesses that fog many people's judgement, and will put his finger on the real problem of the world, i.e. that there is not enough love to go round. Most love is either turned in on itself or restricted to a small selected circle. *A* will point out that Life, Reality, God, and even consideration of their own safety, demand that men should learn to extend the circle of their love and understanding. He will be certain to insist that love toward God does not exist without love to fellow humanity.

4. An endorsement of humanity's own groping

toward truth. For example, true love and self-sacrifice have always been the most deeply moving human characteristics. *A* will probably show that this is because those who truly love and those who give themselves for others are more nearly reflecting the character of God than anyone else.

5. We may reasonably expect *A*'s endorsement also of our appreciation of the loveliness of nature, of the touching grace of childhood and of the wholesome beauty of family life. His ideals will certainly be higher than the finest of ours, but they will not be fantastic or so wholly different from what we already know, as to be unacceptable. The probable reaction of the honest man to *A*'s revelation of the real truth will be: "This rings true. This is what in my secret heart I have always known to be right and real."

6. We need not expect that *A*, like some religious reformers of history, will go about denouncing men as "miserable sinners." Indeed there would be no need of that. Insincerity always feels uncomfortable in the presence of sincerity, unreality in the presence of reality and selfishness in the presence of love. We may expect then that in the presence of a morally complete man, a good deal of spiritual discomfort will be spontaneously aroused, sometimes dully and sometimes acutely. Some men would be stimulated to an intense hunger for wholeness, but some would be angered and resentful and determined either to get

out of range of the cause of their discomfort or to get rid of it.

7. Then we might expect that there will be a conflict with the conventionally religious. *A* is more likely to have trouble here than anywhere, for he will be right up against false gods, self-righteousness, "*quid pro quo*" religion, and particularly those who have divorced religious life from real living, and are now only "playing a part" instead of living life on the human level.

8. We could certainly expect a call to all who will listen, to re-centre their lives on the real God, instead of on things or on themselves. Men, especially worldly-minded men, will probably conclude that *A* is now calling them "miserable sinners" and telling them to "repent." In fact he will be almost imploring them to "look at life differently"—as he knows it really is—with God the centre and all else derived from Him.

VI. IF GOD WERE FOCUSED (II)

ALL THIS, and a great deal more that we can vaguely imagine, would certainly meet *A* and, if he is, as we have supposed, really human, would be heart-breaking. For he would be in the position of a man seeing the truth and yet largely unable to make other men see it. He would see them blind on their God-ward side and drifting farther and farther away from reality. To a sensitive man this would prove an agony: naturally we cannot imagine what it would mean to God-become-man.

We can imagine *A* then as a fully human figure, not floating ethereally in a mystical atmosphere, but with his feet solidly on the earth. His foursquareness to life, his joy in beauty and all good things, his spontaneous love of men and women, will no doubt shock some men as much as his new view-point, standards, and values. They could perhaps tolerate a saintly other-worldly figure, who never sees any harm in anyone, claiming to be God in human form; but for a real man, who seems to be the embodiment of all that is truly human, as well as being quite plainly *en rapport* with the hidden meaning of life, to claim to be God is a very shocking thing. Eyes that penetrate life's little disguises, a tongue that expresses truth in a peculiarly undiluted and memorable form, a personality without the slightest fear and yet quite obviously filled with the highest kind of love—these are formidable things to meet, even for the best of men.

The world frequently conspires to muzzle or destroy its truest seers. The way of the prophet and reformer has usually been hard and not infrequently fatal. There is no reason to suppose that any different fate will be the lot of *A* (always assuming, of course, that he has bound himself not to accept celestial intervention). Indeed, just because *this is It,* real

Truth, real Goodness, real Beauty, real God focused
in human form, it is not unreasonable to imagine
that all the truth-hating and self-loving spiritual
powers will join forces against this unwelcome in-
truder. Misrepresentation, slander, the dead-weight
of age-long custom and authority, false propaganda—
all these weapons will be used against A. He will, if he
proves, as he must, unrepentant and incorruptible,
suffer the full impact of evil. He will probably get
imprisoned, he may even get sentenced to death on
some fantastic charge. If this happened it would, of
course, be an ironical situation without parallel in
the history of the world! God plans and engineers a
Personal visit to His own world, and the reaction of
the world is to get rid of Him!

Of course this is only one side of the picture. There
would probably be many who saw what A was driving
at, and who were deeply stirred by his personality
and life. There would probably be not a few who
would little by little see that his fantastic claim to be
God might well be true. However long or short his
career as a teacher of Truth might be, something of
what he said and did would be memorized or com-
mitted to writing, and even if he were hustled off to
a concentration camp, or judicially murdered, the
truth would remain. Probably a few who really did
see the significance of the human being with whom
they had lived and worked and talked, and who
grasped the enormous value of his teaching to man-

kind, would attempt to tell the world. But without
being unduly cynical, we might reasonably conclude
that a world which would not accept the leader-
ship of God when it was right before their faces in
an understandable form, would not, except for a
small minority, take very seriously the claims of a
handful of devotees of a man who was dead.

VII. HAS *A* ARRIVED?

QUITE A number of people in all parts of the world
have come to the conclusion that the hypothetical *A*
has appeared in history—that *A* in fact equals the
man Jesus, who was born in Palestine some nineteen
centuries ago. Most of the possibilities that we have
suggested might occur if God were to enter this world
humanly, and historically were, they feel reasonably
certain, fulfilled in the life and teaching of Jesus. And
there were some remarkable additional features which
could hardly have been surmised, and which we will
consider in due course.

It is, of course, a very big step intellectually (and
emotionally and morally as well, it will be found) to
accept this famous figure of history as the designed
focusing of God in human life. It is not made any
easier by the clinging mass of sentimentality, super-
stitious reverence, and traditional associations which
surround him. It is emphatically not an easy matter
for the honest modern mind to pierce the accretions

and irrelevancies and see the Person, the Character—particularly as the records, though they have been examined far more closely than any other historic documents, are undeniably meagre. Further, many people who have a vague childish affection for a half-remembered Jesus, have never used their adult critical faculties on the matter at all. They hardly seem to see the paramount importance of His claim to be God. Yet if for one moment we imagine the claim to be true the mind almost reels at its significance. It can only mean that here is Truth, here is the Character of God, the true Design for life, the authentic Yardstick of values, the reliable confirming or correcting of all gropings and inklings about Beauty, Truth, and Goodness, about this world and the next. Life can never be wholly dark or wholly futile if once the key to its meaning is in our hands.

Although an honest adult study of the available records is essential, to decide that Jesus really was the embodiment of God in a human being is not a merely intellectual decision. Our unconscious minds will sense (even if the conscious mind does not) that to accept such a unique Fact cannot but affect the whole of our life. We may with complete detachment study and form a judgement upon a *religion,* but we cannot maintain our detachment if the subject of our inquiry proves to be God Himself. This is, of course, why many otherwise honest intellectual people will construct a neat by-pass around the claim of Jesus to be

God. Being people of insight and imagination, they know perfectly well that once to accept such a claim as fact would mean a readjustment of their own purposes and values and affections which they may have no wish to make. To call Jesus the greatest Figure in History or the finest Moral Teacher the world has ever seen commits no one to anything. But once to allow the startled mind to accept as fact that this man is really focused-God may commit anyone to anything! There is every excuse for blundering in the dark, but in the light there is no cover from reality. It is because we strongly sense this, and not merely because we feel that the evidence is ancient and scanty, that we shrink from committing ourselves to such a far-reaching belief as that Jesus Christ was really God.

But of course we are not entirely at the mercy of our own disinclination to commit ourselves! We want to satisfy our cravings for reality, we want to know the meaning of life and to have spiritual fundamentals upon which we may build a faith by which to live. We want, in short, to know God. Jesus Christ gave three remarkable indications by which men could *know* (not by scientific "proof," but by an inward conviction that is perfectly valid to him in whom it arises) that His claim and His revelation are true. They are contained in three sayings of His which are all well known to anyone even moderately familiar with the Gospels. They are:

(*a*) If any man will do his (i.e. God's) will, he shall know of the doctrine, whether it be of God or whether I speak of myself (JOHN 7¹⁷).

(*b*) He that hath seen me hath seen the Father (JOHN 14⁹).

(*c*) I am the way, the truth, and the life: no man cometh unto the Father, but by me (JOHN 14⁶).

These three sayings, especially the last two, are intolerably arrogant if they come from a purely human moral teacher, but they must inevitably be said by *A* or Jesus Christ if He is really God. Let us consider their significance:

(*a*) Jesus says, in effect, that there will be no inward endorsement of the truth of the way of living he puts forward as the right one until a man is prepared to do the will, i.e. co-operate with the purpose, of God. This at once rules out arm-chair critics of Christianity and any dilettante appraisal of its merits. "You can't know," says Christ, "until you are willing to do."

It is plain from the Gospels that Christ regarded the self-loving, self-regarding, self-seeking spirit as the direct antithesis of real living. His two fundamental rules for life were that the "love-energy," instead of being turned in on itself, should go out first to God and then to other people. "If any man will come after me," he said, "let him deny himself (i.e. deny his tendency to love himself) and take up his cross (i.e. bear the painful cost of that denial) and follow me (i.e. live positively according to the principles that I teach and demonstrate)." Now the moment a man does this, even temporarily and tentatively, he finds himself in touch with something more *real* than he has known before. There is a sense that he is touching a deep and powerful stream that runs right through life. In other words, the moment he begins really to love, he finds himself in touch with the life of God. (And, of course, if God *is* love, this is only to be expected.) He now *knows* beyond any doubting that this is real, happy, constructive living. He knows now that the teaching of Christ is not a merely human code of behaviour, but part of the stuff of reality. He may deliberately seek this way of living, he may touch it by accident or even by force of necessity (as for instance when a selfish husband is shaken out of his selfishness by having to minister to a sick wife): and of course he may relapse into his former way of self-loving. But all the time he was approximating to the living purpose of God he *knew* that this was real life. This, of course, may baffle and even infuriate the detached critic, but it is a pragmatic, universal test whose validity cannot fairly be denied.

(*b*) Christ unquestionably claims to present accurately and authentically the Character of God. As we have seen above, he cannot present the *whole* of God, but he can present in human form a Character that may be understood, admired, loved, respected—or even feared and hated.

Those who accept this claim find that he is the aperture through which the immensity and magnificence of God can be begun to be seen. Nothing that science reveals, nothing that all the complexity of modern thought can demand in its conception of God, either outstrips or outmodes the Character that has been revealed. It would indeed be a mistake to suppose that the eternal God is no "bigger" than Jesus of Nazareth, limited as He was by time and space and circumstance. But the biggest, widest, and highest ideas of God that mind can conceive arrange themselves without dissonance or incongruity around the Character Jesus revealed.

Again we have no scientific "proof" of this. But whereas those who reject the claim of Jesus have to manufacture, and strenuously uphold by continual mental effort, a nebulous God of ultimate values, those who accept the claim find, possibly to their surprise, that without effort God becomes real and "knowable."

(c) If Jesus Christ was God He must say that He is the way, the truth and the life, or words of equivalent meaning, and we find He adds as a matter of unalterable fact that no one comes into contact with God except through Him. This is the third empirical test. Do people in fact know God except through

Christ? It is certainly possible that some stumble on Christ's way of living, even on Christ's Spirit, without realizing quite where they are. But it is very significant that those who reject Christ's claim as fantastic, or even ignore it, *do not know God;* whereas many simple people with little theology or philosophy do find that they "know God" when they give their confidence to the Character that they can trust and love. It is at least possible that a good deal of the scoffing of the superior intellectual at "simple faith" springs from a certain envy. The detached intellectual who will not commit himself knows in his secret heart that he does not know God, indeed may be a million miles from Him for all he knows. Yet the man who has accepted the claim of the "focused God" finds God a living reality, and argument and scorn will, naturally, alike leave him cold.

It is therefore clear that to accept the claim of Christ after proper and careful thought is not entirely a leap into the dark. For the very decision will, as thousands have proved, carry with it an incontrovertible inner endorsement that is worth any amount of argument.

VIII. LIFE'S BASIC PRINCIPLES (I)

IT IS BY no means easy to make an accurate summary of the Character and Truth revealed by Jesus Christ, even if we do not omit those parts of the records which we personally think distasteful or discordant. In this "Christian" country we nearly all have some preconceived, even though vague, idea of the Christ-character and we need to be on our guard against "reading back" into His deeds and words what is already in our minds about Him. Men have tamed and modified and "explained" so much of His message that a great deal of its edge has been blunted. Nor does our reverence for the superb literary quality of the familiar Authorized Version do anything but hinder. Truth that should be regarded as *fact* comes to be regarded as "a beautiful thought": at best it is "a religious truth" rather than a reliable and workable fact on which to act and build. A "fact" of psychological research or of medical science for example is accepted by the mind as being more "true" than a statement of Christ. Yet if Christ was God it should be the other way round.

It may help, therefore, to re-state the basic principles of Jesus Christ in somewhat unfamiliar form.

The truth taught by Jesus Christ is the right way to live. It is not primarily a religion, not even the best religion, but God Himself explaining in terms that men can readily grasp how life is meant to be lived. Naturally, since there is a God and life is His idea, and since "religion" is by definition what connects man and God, there will be a religious flavour to the matter, but we shall fall into a familiar error if we fail to see that Christ is giving direction to the whole of life, and is not Himself, as we so often are, dividing off a particular section and calling it "religious."

If we accept Christ's claim to be God we have a right to expect that certain basic facts will be told us on His authority, so that at any rate it becomes possible for us to be intelligent and willing co-operators with that whole Scheme of Things which we call Life. Here then are our basic requirements, put into the form of simple questions:

1. *What sort of Person is God?*

Christ's answer is quite unequivocal. He is "the Father." When we hear this familiar truth we nearly always read back into God's Character what we know of fatherhood. This is understandable enough, but it reverses the actual truth. If God is "the Father," in Nature and Character and Operation, then we derive (if we are parents) our characteristics from Him. We are reproducing, no doubt on a microscopic scale and in a thoroughly faulty manner, something of the Character of God. If once we accept it as true that the whole Power behind this astonishing universe is of that kind of character that Christ could only describe as "Father," the whole of life is transfigured. If we are really seeing in human relationships fragmentary and faulty but real reflections of the Nature of God, a flood of light is immediately released upon all the life that we can see. People, and our relationships with them, at once become of tremendous importance. Much of life is seen to be merely its setting, its stage, its "props"—the *business* of it is in the realm of personality: it is people not things that matter. It is thus quite impossible to divorce Christianity from life. Those who attempted to divorce the religion of their day from ordinary life were called by Christ, "play-actors" (hypocrites), i.e. they were acting a part and not really living at all.

2. *What is the purpose of Life?*

Christ did not give an answer to this question in its modern cynical form which implies, "Is it worth living at all?" but He did answer those who wanted to know what to do with the vitality, affections, and talents, with which they were endowed. He also answered those who already saw intuitively that this present life was transitory and incomplete and wanted to know how to be incorporated into the main timeless Stream of Life itself. The questions are really much the same. In both cases men wanted to know how they could be at one with Life's real purpose. And of course they still do. He said that there were really two main principles of living on which all true morality and wisdom might be said to depend. The first was to love God with the whole of a man's personality, and the second to love his fellow men as much and in the same way as he naturally loved himself. If these two principles were obeyed Christ said that a man would be in harmony with the Purpose of Life, which transcends time.

These two principles, one of which deals with the Invisible and Unchanging, the other with the visible and variable, cover the total relationships of a man's life. Christ made them intensely practical and indissolubly connected. The expression of love for God did not lie in formal piety nor in mystical contemplation, but in obedience to what he believed to be the will of God, which very often meant, in fact, the succouring and service of other men. A man could not be "friends with" God on any other terms than complete obedience to Him, and that included being "friends with" his fellow men. Christ stated emphatically that it was quite impossible in the nature of things for a man to be at peace with God and at variance with his neighbour. This disquieting fact is often hushed up, but it is undeniable that Christ said it, and the truth of it is enshrined (or should we say more properly embalmed) in the petition for forgiveness in the all-too-familiar "Lord's Prayer."

The purpose of Life would seem to be the gradual winning of men to a willing loyalty to these two principles, the establishing of the Rule of God. Christ labelled the first one "primary and most important," probably because unless principles and values are first established by loving the true God there will not be "enough love to go round." The world would go on loving its own selected circle, despising, exploiting or hating those outside it unless their hearts were first attuned to "the Father." Those who have exalted the second principle to the neglect of the first have again and again proved the wisdom of Christ's choice of their order.

IX. LIFE'S BASIC PRINCIPLES (II)

3. *What is Really Wrong with the World?*

THIS IS an extremely important question if only because it is asked so often and answered in so many different ways. Christ answered it, not directly, but quite plainly by implication. It is here, in diagnosis, that it is perhaps most important of all to realize the paramount authority of what Christ said. None of us thinks or speaks or feels without bias, and all of us are prone to fit facts to a theory. Christ had no bias and no theory: He came to give us the facts, and they are quite plainly, that this "power-to-love" which He recommended should be expended on God and other people, has been turned in on itself. The basic problems of happiness are not intellectual, but emotional. It is "out of the heart," according to Christ, that there proceed all those things which spoil relationships whether between individuals or between groups of people.

It is obvious, if we accept Christ's two great principles, that "sin" will lie in the refusal to follow them.

To Christ the most serious sin was not the misdirec-
tion of the love-energy, which might be due to
ignorance or mere carelessness, but the deliberate
refusal to allow it to flow out either to God or to other
people. This accounts for some of His surprising reversals of conventional moral judgement. It was pride
and self-righteousness and the exploitation of others
which called forth His greatest anger. Self-love in fact
He saw as the arch-enemy. It was this which must be
recognized and deliberately killed if a man were to
follow His way of constructive love.

A few moments' thought will show us how true
was His insight. While there is no "sin" that we can
name which does not spring from love of self, yet the
sins which do most damage and cause most suffering
are those which have the highest content of self-love.

Christ's time, in the circumstances, was short and
He wasted none of it in dealing with mere symptoms.
It was with the motive and attitude of the heart, i.e.
the emotional centre, that He was concerned. It
was this that He called on men to change, for it is
plain that once the inner affections are aligned with
God the outward expression of the life will look after
itself.

4. *What sort of people does God intend men to be?*

To this question Christ gave an explicit answer which,
if considered seriously, is a real shock to the mind. He

gave a complete reversal of conventional values and ambitions, though many people miss this undoubted fact because of the poetic form and archaic language of what are now called the "Beatitudes." Their revolutionary character becomes apparent at once, however, if we substitute the word "happy" for the word "blessed" (which is perfectly fair), and if we paraphrase the familiar cadences of the Authorized Version and put the thoughts more into the form in which we normally accept facts and definitions. We may further throw their real character into relief by contrasting each "beatitude" with the normal view of the man of the world throughout the centuries. We can do it lik this:

Most people think:

Happy are the pushers: for they get on in the world.

Happy are the hard-boiled: for they never let life hurt them.

Happy are they who complain: for they get their own way in the end.

Happy are the blasé: for they never worry over their sins.

Happy are the slave-drivers: for they get results.

Happy are the knowledgeable men of the world: for they know their way around.

Happy are the trouble-makers: for people have to take notice of them.

Jesus Christ said:

*Happy are those who realize their spiritual poverty:
they have already entered the kingdom of
Reality.*

*Happy are they who bear their share of the world's
pain: in the long run they will know more happiness than those who avoid it.*

*Happy are those who accept life and their own
limitations: they will find more in life than
anybody.*

*Happy are those who long to be truly "good":
they will fully realize their ambition.*

*Happy are those who are ready to make allowances
and to forgive: they will know the love of God.*

*Happy are those who are real in their thoughts and
feelings: in the end they will see the ultimate
Reality, God.*

*Happy are those who help others to live together:
they will be known to be doing God's work.*

It is quite plain that Christ is setting up ideals of
different quality from those commonly accepted. He
is outlining the sort of human characteristics which
may fairly be said to be co-operating with the purpose
of Life, and He is by implication exposing the conventional mode of living which is at heart based on
self-love and leads to all kinds of unhappiness.

It should be noticed that this "recipe" for happy
and constructive living is of universal application. It

cuts across differences of temperament and variations in capacity. It outlines the kind of character which is possible for *any* man, gifted or relatively ungifted, strong or weak, clever or slow in the uptake. Once more we find Christ placing His finger not upon the externals, but upon the vital internal attitude.

It should also be noted that although we have called His definitions "revolutionary" they are not fantastic. Indeed a great many people would probably realize that in following them men would become their real selves and not the greedy, competitive, self-loving characters that cause so many of the world's troubles. Christ is restoring the true order, which man can recognize as true, He is not imposing a set of arbitrary regulations.

5. *What are we to make of pain and disease,*
   injustice and evil?

We find Christ accepting these things, which many people advance as the greatest hindrance to religious faith, as part of the stuff of life. He did not pretend that they do not exist: He coped with them personally by restoring, wherever possible, the true order of health, sanity, and constructive goodness. He made no promise that those who followed Him in His plan of re-establishing life on its proper basic principles would enjoy special immunity from pain and sorrow —nor did He Himself experience such immunity. He did, however, promise enough joy and courage, enough love and confidence in God to enable those who went His way to do far more than survive. Because they would be in harmony with the very Life and Spirit of God they would be able to defeat evil. They would be able to take the initiative and destroy evil with good.

Although Christ gave no explicit explanation of the existence of pain and evil in the world, He gave certain implied facts which are well worth our serious consideration.

(a) The "breaking of the rules" means suffering. The operation of self-love on a huge scale, which means a wholesale breaking of His two fundamental rules for human life, cannot but mean a highly complex and widespread "infection" of suffering. Men are not isolated units and their every action in some degree affects other people. The multiplication of the effects of countless acts by millions of self-centred, instead of God-centred, individuals may reasonably be thought to be destroying the world. The only way of being rescued from the vicious sin-suffering-death circle in which the world is involved is for men to re-centre their lives on God. This they can do by deliberately giving their confidence to the Character which Christ exhibited in person and thereby seeing that real living, in harmony with God, lies in following Him and His basic principles.

There is thus no easy answer to the evil and suffering problem and no easy road to its solution. But

Christ tackled the matter radically and realistically by winning the allegiance of a few men and women to a new way of living. Most people, he said, were drifting along the broad road of conventional standards which has in it the threat of destruction. The narrow road of following the basic rules which, because it is in harmony with God, is not affected by what we call death, was being followed by comparatively few. His plan of rescue (or salvation, to use a much misused word) had to begin with a tiny minority. They were to be the spear-head of good against evil.

(*b*) Christ definitely spoke of a power of spiritual evil, and, using the language of His contemporaries, He called this power "Satan," "the Devil," or "the Evil One." Now whatever mystery lies behind the existence of such an evil spiritual power—whether we accept a Miltonic idea of a fallen angelic power or whether we conceive the evil spirit in the world as arising out of the cumulative effects of centuries of selfish living—there can be no blinking the fact that Christ spoke, and acted, on the assumption that there is a power of evil operating in the world. If we accept as fact His claim to be God this must make us think seriously.

We are so accustomed by modern thought to regard evil as "error," as the "growing pains" of civilization, or simply as an inexplicable problem, that once more the mind does not readily accept what is in effect

God's own explanation—that there is a spirit of evil operating in the world. We find Christ speaking quite plainly of this spirit as responsible for disease and insanity as well as being the unremitting enemy of those who want to follow the new, true order.

Modern man has a lust for full explanation and habitually considers himself in no way morally bound unless he is in full possession of all the facts. Hence, of course, the prevalence of non-committal agnosticism. Yet it would seem that Christ, God-become-Man, did not give men a full explanation of the origin and operation of the evil forces in this world. (It is perfectly possible that in our present space-time existence we could not comprehend it, anyway.) But He did recognize evil as evil, not as a mere absence of good: He did, wherever He found it possible, destroy evil. He did indicate the lines along which evil could be defeated and He did talk of the positive resources which would be necessary for such defeat, and these we must consider a little later.

X. FURTHER BASIC QUESTIONS

What is the truth about sin and forgiveness?

SOONER or later this question in some form or other must be asked and answered. For the problem of imperfect man's safe approach to the Moral Perfection of God is the business of every religion worthy of the name. Because most people in this modern age have almost no sense of God there is also almost no sense of "sin"—for in human experience there is a significant connexion between the two. Where the sense of God becomes something like a reality there springs up, sooner or later, a sense of guilt and failure. This is equally true of the most primitive as well as of the most highly developed religions of mankind. And where there is this sense of sin there is a deeply rooted conviction that "something ought to be done about it." Animal, even human, sacrifices, propitiatory offerings of various kinds and acts of ceremonial cleansing—all testify to the desire to "do something" to bridge the moral gulf between the holiness of God and the sinfulness of man.

A great deal of sentimental (i.e. unreal) stuff has been spoken and written about the matter of sin and forgiveness, and we must therefore clear our minds a little more before we see the significance of what Christ had to say about this very important subject. Let us start, then, by making these observations.

1. *We are not concerned with "artificial" guilt or sin.*

In the first part of this book we considered how conscience could make a man feel guilty simply because certain standards and taboos had been established in his mind and he had failed to "toe the line." All religions, Christianity unfortunately not excepted, tend to excite in certain people this artificial sense

of guilt, which may have little or no connexion with
a man's actual standing before God. Probably Pharisaism, which Christ attacked with bitter scorn, represents this tendency at its highest, but it is a mistake
to think that Pharisaism disappeared after the death
of Christ. The danger of such a system, and the reason
why Christ attacked it so violently, is that its values
are artificial. The proud and correct feel "right with
God" just when they are not, and the sensitive humble
man feels hopeless and overburdened *for the wrong
reasons*. (Christ's little cameo of the Pharisee and the
tax-collector at their prayers is an unforgettable com-
mentary on this point.)

2. *We are not concerned with mere comparison
   with perfection.*

We have already spoken in the first part of this book
of the dangers of worshipping "one hundred per
cent" as God. A great deal of the sense of sin and
shame and guilt induced in certain types of people
is simply due to their (imaginary) comparison of their
human standards with what they conceive to be the
Divine Standards. Of course they feel failures! You
have only to raise the standard, and go on raising it,
to make anyone feel a hopeless blundering idiot.
This may be what we are in comparison with the
wisdom of God, but, to put it at its crudest, it would
be an extraordinarily ungentlemanly thing for Him
merely to keep raising the standard! After all, it is a

foregone conclusion that no man can compete with his Creator, and there is neither sense nor justice in thinking that the Creator intends His creatures to feel permanently inferior and humiliated compared with Himself! Yet this comparison, cloaked and disguised, is often made in a certain type of sermon and a certain type of religious book. But the feeling of hopelessness and inadequacy it engenders is quite wrongly taken to be "conviction of sin."

3. *We are not concerned with mere humiliation.*

Quite a lot of people, if psychologically tested, would react with resentment to the words "sin," "guilt," "disobedience," "punishment," and so on. This is by no means necessarily because their adult lives are so proud and complacent that they resent criticism, but because there still exists in their minds a tender, touchy area connected with the misdemeanours of childhood. Unless they were exceptionally lucky it is quite probable that, though they have long ago forgotten the circumstances, they still half-consciously remember the shame, rage, impotence, and humiliation of childish naughtiness and its punishment. It was not without strain and conflict that they won free from adult domination, and it *feels* to them like a voluntary resumption of the humiliations of childhood to confess themselves "guilty sinners." For a little boy to be smacked on his behind may be of little significance, but for an adult man to be beaten is an unspeakable degradation. It is of course not really a renascence of this childish guilt and humiliation that the reputable evangelist seeks to arouse, but he may seem to be doing so. To have a real sense of sin is by no means the same thing as being humiliated.

The true adult sense of sin, guilt, and shame, which contact with the real God appears invariably to arouse (though by no means always at once), seems to come along at least four different lines, which we will attempt to illustrate.

(*a*) We will suppose that a man who is rather proud of his ability to knock off a quick effective little painting discovers a bit of canvas fastened to a wall. For his own pleasure and the appreciation of his friends he rapidly paints in a bright, effective, and amusing little picture. Stepping back to see his own handiwork better he suddenly discovers that he has painted his little bit of nonsense on the corner of a vast painting of superb quality, so huge that he had not realized its extent or even that there was a picture there at all. His feelings are rather like what a man feels when he suddenly sees the vast sweep of God's design in life, and observes the cheap and discordant little effort his own living so far represents when seen against that background. That is real conviction of sin.

(*b*) To illustrate the second way in which a real sense of sin may come, we will use a story which we believe is true, though it has not been possible to check its source. A young man of the "incorrigible" variety grows up work-shy, and by a certain native quickness of wit manages for years to escape serious trouble. His favourite saying is: "I live my own life, and I don't care tuppence for anybody." Eventually, however, his self-confidence overreaches itself and he is convicted of serious crime and goes to prison for three years. While in prison he is hard and quite unrepentant. "What I do with my life," he says defiantly, "is nobody else's business. I shan't make the same mistake twice." In due course he leaves prison and, since he has nowhere else to go, decides to spend a few nights at home while he "looks around." He hasn't seen his mother since he saw her, plump, rosy, and tearful, out of the corner of his eye, at his trial. But when the door of his home is opened to him by a worn, grey-haired old woman, he does not see at once what has happened. For a second or two he simply stares, then he cries, "Oh, mother, what *have I done to you?*" and bursts into the tears that neither punishment nor prison had ever wrung from him.

This story is simply an illustration of how a man may suddenly realize the hurt he does to others by his own self-centredness. It does not, unfortunately, often happen that a man sees as vividly as in that story the consequences of his wrong actions. But when he does he may experience a genuine conviction of sin. When Saul Kane in Masefield's *Everlasting Mercy* had his eyes opened, he suddenly saw "the

harm I done in being me." That is just it. When a
man sees not merely that his life is out of harmony
with God's purpose, but realizes that that disharmony
has injured and infected the lives of other people,
he begins to feel a "sinner" in earnest.

(c) To illustrate the next point we must tell a
simple story which will no doubt make the sophisti-
cated smile. Two young men of the same age choose
divergent paths. A is determined to squeeze all the
pleasure and enjoyment out of life that he can. B is
equally determined to "get on." Despite the gibes
of his friend, he attends "evening classes" and works
hard in his spare time at his chosen subject. We will
suppose that the friends go separate ways and do not
meet for several years. When they do B has unquestionably "got on" and has a responsible well-paid
position. A has advanced very little. His reaction on
seeing B again may quite possibly be just unreasonable envy, but equally possibly A may say to himself: "What a fool I've been! What opportunities I
threw away. B is *just the sort of man I could have
been!*"

This naïve little tale illustrates quite well how a
genuine "conviction of sin" may arise. A man who
has lived selfishly and carelessly meets someone who
has plainly found happiness and satisfaction in co-
operating with what he can see of God's purpose. The
former may pass the whole thing off as a joke. "Of
course, old so-and-so always was a bit religious"—but

he may quite possibly see in the other man *the sort of person he himself might have been.* The standards he mocked and the God he kept at arm's length have produced in the other man something he really very badly wants. If his reflection is, "What a fool I've been," he, too, is beginning to get a genuine sense of sin.

(d) The fourth road along which the "conviction of sin" may come is rather harder to explain. It is really the discovery of the enormous and implacable strength of real goodness and real love. The insincere man hates and fears the real truth: the sexually irresponsible man affects to be cynical about real and enduring passion, but secretly he hates and fears it: the egocentric man hates and fears the incalculable force of the personality selflessly devoted to a cause. In short, self-centred and evil people really *fear* the good. They express their fear by mockery, cynicism, and, when circumstances allow, by active persecution.

Now when this sense of the strength of goodness and love touches a man, whether it be by someone else's life, by something he reads or sees, or by an inner touch in his soul, he is really convicted of sin. He knows that sooner or later the game is up—the Nature of Life is Good and not Evil. He suddenly sees that the goodness and love he has despised as weakness are in reality incredibly strong. Peter once felt this about Christ and in a moment of panic cried out: "Depart from me, for I am a sinful man, O

Lord!" Some people, of course, succeed in keeping the fear of goodness (which is really the fear of God) at a safe distance all their lives, but they live in continual danger of reality breaking in. And when it does there will be a strong sense of sin.

XI. CHRIST AND THE QUESTION OF SIN

THERE ARE, of course, several other genuine ways in which a man feels a moral failure before God. But however he may arrive at the point of realization he will, sooner or later, realize what may be described as the bankruptcy of his position. He sees, for instance, that his life has done harm to others, that he has spoiled the Design, that he has played the fool with a good deal of his life. He realizes, dimly perhaps, that he has offended against the Order of Things. Yet there is nothing very much he can do about it. He can be sorry, and he can apologize. He can resolve to do better in future. But if his sense of sin is more than superficial he will feel two things. First that some *rapprochement* must be made between his sinful self and the moral perfection of God (and here he may feel a passing sympathy with the almost universal idea of sacrifice found in primitive religions). Secondly, he will need some assuring that he can be, and is, accepted into fellowship with God. He wants, desperately sometimes, to be in harmony with the meaning and purpose of life, and yet he feels helpless

CHRIST AND THE QUESTION OF SIN   115

to "make the atonement" that he senses is necessary.

To anyone therefore who takes the unique claim of Christ seriously it is of the very greatest interest and significance to observe how He dealt with the question of sin and man's reconciliation with God. The following facts emerge from the records:

(1) Christ very rarely called men "sinners" and as far as we know never attempted deliberately to make them feel sinners, except in the case of the entrenched self-righteous, where He used the assault and battery of scathing denunciation. (This, we may surmise, is an instance of what He saw to be a desperate ill requiring a desperate remedy.) Some evangelists, whose chief weapon is the production of a sense of sin, would find themselves extraordinarily short of ammunition if they were obliged to use nothing but the recorded words of Christ. This is not, of course, to say that the life and words of Christ did not produce that genuine sense of guilt and failure which is outlined above, but it is undeniable that He did not set out to impress a sense of sin on His hearers.

(2) We find Christ unequivocally claiming the right "to forgive sins," but the grounds on which the sin of man can be forgiven are not, in the recorded words of Christ, the conventional ones presupposed by many Christians. We find in Christ an intimate connexion between the forgiveness of sins and the existence of love in a man's heart. "Forgive us our trespasses as we forgive them that trespass against us"

is so familiar in our ears that we hardly grasp the fact that Christ joined fellowship with God and fellowship with other human beings indissolubly. "Except ye from your hearts forgive everyone his trespasses," He is reported to have said after a particularly telling parable, "neither will my heavenly Father forgive you your trespasses." Moreover, on one occasion he said of a woman who was apparently something of a notoriety that "her sins, *which are many,* are forgiven: for she loved much." It seems to me consonant with Christ's teaching to hold that love is a prerequisite of forgiveness, and I take His consequent little story to the Pharisee to be another of those apparent "non sequiturs" of which the reply to the question "Who is my neighbour?" is a classic example.

On the other hand, it would seem that there is a possibility of a man's putting himself outside forgiveness by the "sin against the Holy Spirit." This, from an examination of the context, would appear to be a combination of refusing to recognize truth and refusing to allow the heart to love others. If God Himself is both Truth and Love it would be logical to suppose that a deliberate refusal to recognize or harbour truth and love would result in an attitude that makes reconciliation with God impossible.

Now if it is true that God is both Truth and Love it will readily be seen that the greatest sins will be unreality, hypocrisy, deceit, lying, or whatever else we choose to call sins against truth, and self-love, which makes fellowship with other people and their proper treatment impossible. Forgiveness must then consist in a restoration to Reality, i.e. Truth and Love.

(3) We must now ask whether Christ had anything to say about the clamant question of "atonement" mentioned above. He certainly hinted at it. He spoke of giving his life as "a ransom for many," and at the last meal which He shared with His followers He spoke of breaking His own body and shedding His own blood "for the remission of sins."

Now it is surely possible that to this question of atonement (as to the question of surviving death) Christ, whom we are considering as God in human form, could give the best and most complete answer by actual demonstration. He personally, being both God and Man, effected the reconciliation that man alone was powerless to make.

There are innumerable theories centring around the death of Christ as the atonement for the world's sins, and many of them frankly do not commend themselves to the honest modern mind. May we suggest the following way of looking at the matter.

We have already spoken of the vicious sin-suffering-death circle in which the world is involved, and of the individual man's helplessness to free himself from the entanglement of his own wrong-doing, let alone cleanse himself from the cumulative infection of the world's selfish living.

Suppose now that God, who has become human and represents in one person both His own Godhood and Humanity, allows Himself, though personally guiltless, to be involved in the complex. God, now, who made the inexorable rules of cause and effect, deliberately exposes Himself to the consequences of the world's self-love and sin. Because He is God, to do such a thing once in time is indicative of an eternal attitude, and we view the Character of God in an entirely different light if we see Him not abrogating justice, not issuing a mandate of reversal of natural law and order, but overcoming a repugnance which we cannot begin to imagine by letting Himself *be* Representative Man and suffering in His own Person the logical and inevitable suffering and death which the world has earned. The Moral Perfection which a man quite rightly dreads, has deliberately consented to become under the limitations of humanity, the focal point of the assault of evil. We cannot imagine what this would involve, but even to begin to think that it might be true takes the breath away.

Christians believe that this act of reconciliation was the inner meaning behind the rather sordid historical fact of Christ's death. The unreality, the pseudo-religion, the bitter hatred, the greed and jealousy that lay behind the judicial murder of Christ were the mere *setting*. The *fact* would have been the same wherever and whenever Christ appeared: evil would clash with Incarnate Good, and whether it was a cross, a hangman's rope, a guillotine, or a gas-chamber, Christ would choose to accept death for humanity's sake.

XII. SATISFACTORY RECONCILIATION

WE SHALL attempt here no theories of atonement, but simply record that it is a matter of indisputable fact that when a man sees that God took the initiative in establishing a *rapprochement* between Himself and Man and underwent the (for Him) indescribable ignominy of death, his attitude toward God is from then on profoundly changed. The inarticulate but incurable sense that "something ought to be done about it," to which we referred above, is almost miraculously set at rest. Though it may defeat his reason to define exactly what has been done, a man knows that the "something" has been done. The idea of God, which was almost certainly a discomfort and possibly a threat, however reason might argue the point, is entirely changed. The former inevitable Judge is seen to be Lover and Rescuer, and if the revision of ideas is at all sudden there is bound to be a considerable emotional release.

To assent mentally to the suggestion that "Jesus died for me" is unhappily only too easy for certain types of mind. But really to believe that God Himself cut the knot of man's entanglement by a personal and unbelievably costly act is a much deeper

affair. The bigger the concept of God the more the
mind staggers at the thought, but once it is accepted
as true it is not too much to say that the whole personality is reorientated. For most men in whom a
moral sense is operating at all, are, unconsciously
perhaps, trying to "put up a case" to justify their
own conduct. The effort may only rarely reach the
conscious level of the mind, but it is there, and the
real "conviction of sin" which we defined above, however much it may be held at arm's length, is always
in the offing. To realize that the effort to justify one-
self, the hopeless effort to repay the overdraft, can
safely be abandoned, is an unspeakable relief. It was
all based on a false idea, that the central confidence
of life should be in the self. It is a blow to the face
of pride and a wrench to the habits of the mind to
transfer that central confidence to the One Real
Perfect Man, who was, and is, also God. But if the
change-over is effected the relief and release are
enormous, and energy formerly repressed is set free.
This is what the New Testament means by being
saved by faith in Christ.

This is, of course, far from being mere theory.
People in all ages, of all nations, and of widely differ-
ing temperaments, have reacted in much the same
way to Christ's Act of Reconciliation. Indeed so great
is the weight of evidence that it would be sensible
to admit that, if we cannot understand what happened and are at a loss to explain it, there is a

mystery here beyond our powers of definition. We might even have the humility to say that God-become-man did something incalculable, the greatness of which we can only appreciate in a very limited degree.

But, though we may well be awed, we need not cease to use our minds, and we cannot but admire the superb psychological accuracy with which this Act was designed to touch the characters of men. Those who already to some extent live in love and truth will see the force and point of the Act almost intuitively. Those who are set, however secretly, in pride and self-love, will see nothing to marvel at and little to admire—though the Act may haunt them strangely as though it were the key to some long-forgotten door into life's real meaning. It is those who realize their spiritual poverty who find in Christ's Act the way into fellowship with God: it is the "rich" who are "turned empty away."

Nevertheless, although we have here a touchstone to reveal existing character, we have a great deal more than that. Should the proud and self-loving man once see that God is *like that*, there may be, and sometimes is, a revolution in his whole scale of values. Should the careless-living man once see that this Act is a crystallizing in time of what is always happening—that every kind of sin, including apathy, is at heart seeking to destroy God—he too may see life with very different eyes. God may thunder His commands from Mount Sinai and men may fear, yet remain at

heart exactly as they were before. But let a man once
see his God down in the arena as a Man, suffering,
tempted, sweating, and agonized—finally dying a
criminal's death, he is a hard man indeed who is un-
touched. For Christ's claim to be not only God but
Representative Man has had an almost incredible
magnetic power. Over nineteen centuries have passed
since that judicial murder in that turbulent little
country of Palestine, yet still men see the Death as a
personal matter. It seems to be designed to meet their
own half-conscious needs. "The Son of God who
loved *me* and gave Himself for *me*," wrote St. Paul,
as though for the moment the Act affected him alone;
but the words have been echoed unprompted by an
imposing number since his day. So wide has been the
acceptance of this reconciliation that we simply cannot easily dismiss it, particularly as the only possible
alternative way of thought is a simple denial of the
impasse which is a "fact" to every spiritually sensitive person.

XIII. DEMONSTRATION WITH THE ENEMY

WE HAVE mentioned above that Jesus Christ did not,
as far as we know, say a great deal about the question
of sin and its forgiveness, but gave a complete and
satisfactory answer by personal demonstration. The
same thing is true of His reply to the other question
which has always been in men's minds: "Is there life

after death?" For although in His recorded teaching the existence of a real world, unaffected by time and space, is assumed, the complete and satisfactory answer to the question of whether a human being could survive the universal experience of death was given by personal demonstration. An observed historical fact, as in the case of the Act of Reconciliation, provided the most effective reply to mankind's questioning.

It is, of course, impossible to exaggerate the importance of the historicity of what is commonly known as the Resurrection. If, after all His claims and promises, Christ had died and merely lived on as a fragrant memory, He could only be revered as an extremely good but profoundly mistaken man. His claims to be God, His claims to be Himself the very principle of Life, would be mere self-delusion. His authoritative pronouncements on the nature of God and Man and Life would be at once suspect. Why should He be right about the lesser things if He was proved completely wrong in the greater?

It is perfectly natural therefore that both Christians and anti-Christians should regard the question of whether the Resurrection really took place as the fundamental issue on which the whole Christian claim really depends. Argument on both sides has been continuous and vehement for centuries, and it is not very likely that at this distance from the event any fresh evidence, or even fresh opinion, will emerge.

It does not seem to be a matter that can be finally settled by the most careful study or the most ingenious argument. The very lack of chronological arrangement and careful mutual endorsement that characterizes the stories of the Resurrection appears to one side as evidence of their slipshod and even imaginative nature, while to the other the same things seem to be the ingenuousness of those who were so convinced of what they had seen that they had no need to build up a foolproof body of evidence. Again, the fact that the recorded appearances were made only to those who were "on Jesus' side" is enough for one group to conclude that they are of purely subjective value, while for the other it is plain proof that only those who are at heart reconciled to God can even see the reality of Life once it is detached from the present space-time limitations.

We do not propose, therefore, to attempt to marshal the arguments on one side or the other, but merely to ask three questions which must in fairness be answered if the historical fact of the Resurrection is rejected.

1. *What changed the early disciples?*

No fair reading of the records can deny that almost all the disciples of Jesus deserted Him at the disaster of the Crucifixion, and that afterwards, with their Leader dead and their hopes at zero, they were living in considerable personal apprehension. Yet within a very short time we find them, quite a considerable body of men, filled with an extraordinary courage and spiritual vitality, defying the power of both pagan and Jewish authorities. They are proclaiming openly that they had themselves seen Jesus alive, not once, but several times, after His public execution, and calling all men to share their belief that this Man was indeed God. Nor was this a short-lived spurt of defiant courage, but a steady flame of conviction which baffled, embarrassed, and infuriated the authorities for years as the movement began to spread throughout the then-known world. It is surely straining credulity to bursting point to believe that this dramatic and sustained change of attitude was founded on hallucination, hysteria, or an ingenious swindle. We may thoroughly disapprove of the Christian faith, but it is impossible to deny that the early Christians quite definitely believed that they had seen, touched, handled, and conversed with Christ after He had been crucified, taken down, and laid in a rock-hewn vault sealed and guarded by Roman soldiers.

2. *If the Resurrection did not happen, who was Christ?*

Many people, who have not read the Gospels since childhood, imagine that they can quite easily detach the "miraculous" element of the Resurrection and still retain Christ as an Ideal, as the best Moral

Teacher the world has ever known—and all the rest. But the gospels, all four of them, bristle with supernatural claims on the part of Christ, and unless each man is going to constitute himself a judge of what Christ said and what He did not say (which is not far from every man being his own evangelist), it is impossible to avoid the conclusion that He believed Himself to be God and spoke therefore with quite unique authority. Now if He believed thus and spoke thus and failed to rise from the dead, He was, without question, a lunatic. He was quite plainly a young idealist suffering from *folie de grandeur* on the biggest possible scale, and cannot on that account be regarded as the World's Greatest Teacher. No Mahomet or Buddha or other great teacher ever came within miles of making such a shocking boast about himself. Familiarity has blinded many people to the outrageousness of Christ's claim and traditional reverence inhibits them from properly assessing it. If He did not in fact rise, His claim was false, and He was a very dangerous personality indeed.

3. *Why are so many Christians sure that Christ not only rose, but is alive today?*

Though this question may enrage the critic it is a fair one. The common experience of Christians of all kinds of temperaments and of a great many nationalities for nineteen centuries cannot be airily dismissed. Men and women by the thousand today are convinced

that the One whom they serve is not a heroic figure
of the past, but a living Personality with spiritual resources upon which they can draw. A man may find
difficulty in writing a poem, but if he cries, "Oh,
William Shakespeare, help me!" nothing whatever
happens. A man may be terribly afraid, but if he cries,
"Oh, Horatio Nelson, help me!" there is no sort of
reply. But if he is at the end of his moral resources
or cannot by effort of will muster up sufficient positive love and goodness and he cries, "Oh, Christ, help
me!" something happens at once. The sense of spiritual reinforcement, of drawing spiritual vitality from
a living source, is so marked that Christians cannot
help being convinced that their Hero is far more than
an outstanding figure of the past.

The fact that this conviction only comes to those
who have centred their inner confidence on Jesus
Christ seems to rob it of all validity in the eyes of
the hostile critic. Yet if, by an effort of imagination
such a critic would concede for a moment that the
claims of Christ were true, he must admit that the
phenomenon is logical. If Christ revealed the true
way of living and offered human beings the possibility
of being in harmony with the Life of God (i.e.
"eternal life"), it must follow that anyone living in
any other way is by that continued action incapable
of appreciating the quality of real living unless and
until he "takes the plunge" into it. A man may write
and argue and even write poems about human love,

but he does not *know* love until he is in it, and even then his knowledge of it only grows as he discards his self-love and accepts the pains and responsibilities as well as the joys of loving someone else.

"If any man will *know* whether my teaching is human or divine truth," said Christ, "let him *do* the will of God." Those who accept this penetrating challenge are convinced that Christ is alive.

XIV. THE ABOLITION OF DEATH

THE "FOCUSED" God, Jesus Christ, revealed to man not merely adequate working-instructions for meeting life happily and constructively, but also the means by which he could be linked with the timeless Life of God. "Heaven" is not, so to speak, the reward for "being a good boy" (though many people seem to think so), but is the continuation and expansion of a quality of life which begins when a man's central confidence is transferred from himself to God-become-man. This "faith" links him here and now with truth and love, and it is significant that Jesus Christ on more than one occasion is reported to have spoken of "eternal life" as being entered into *now,* though plainly to extend without limitation after the present incident that we call life. The man who believes in the authenticity of His message and puts his confidence in it already possesses the quality of "eternal life" (John 3^{36}, 5^{24}, 6^{47}, etc.). He comes to bring men

not merely "life," but life of a deeper and more enduring quality (John 10^{10}, 10^{28}, 17^3, etc.).

If we accept this we shall not be too surprised to
find Christ teaching an astonishing thing about
physical death: not merely that it is an experience
robbed of its terror, but that as an experience *it does
not exist at all.* For some reason or other Christ's
words (which Heaven knows are taken literally
enough when men are trying to prove a point about
pacifism or divorce, for example) are taken with
more than a pinch of salt when He talks about the
common experience of death as it affects the man
whose basic trust is in Himself: "If a man keep my
saying *he shall never see death*" (John 8^{51}); "Whoso-
ever liveth and believeth on Me *shall never die*"
(John 11^{26}). It is impossible to avoid the conclusion
that the meaning that Christ intended to convey was
that death was a completely negligible experience to
the man who had already begun to live life of the
eternal quality.

"Jesus Christ hath abolished death," wrote Paul
many years ago, but there have been very few since
his day who appear to have believed it. The power
of the dark old god, rooted no doubt in instinctive
fear, is hard to shake, and a great many Christian
writers, though possessing the brightest hopes of "Life
Hereafter" cannot, it seems, accept the abolition of
death. "The valley of the shadow," "Death's gloomy
portal," "the bitter pains of death," and a thousand

other expressions all bear witness to the fact that a
vast number of Christians do not really believe what
Christ said. Probably the greatest offender is John
Bunyan, writing in his *Pilgrim's Progress* of the icy
river through which the pilgrims must pass before
they reach the Celestial City. Thousands, possibly
millions, must have been influenced in their impres-
sionable years by reading *Pilgrim's Progress*. Yet the
"icy river" is entirely a product of Bunyan's own
fears, and the New Testament will be searched in
vain for the slightest endorsement of his idea. To
"sleep in Christ," "to depart and be with Christ,"
"to fall asleep"—these are the expressions the New
Testament uses. It is high time the "icy river," "the
gloomy portal," "the bitter pains," and all the rest
of the melancholy images were brought face to face
with the fact: "Jesus Christ hath abolished death."

The fact seems to many to be too good to be true.
But if it does seem so, it is because we have not really
accepted the revolutionary character of God's personal
entry into the world. Once it dawns upon us that
God (incredible as it may well sound) has actually
identified Himself with Man, that He has taken the
initiative in effecting the necessary Reconciliation of
Man with Himself, and has shown the way by which
little human personalities can begin to embark on
that immense adventure of Living of which God is
the Centre, death—the discarding of a temporary ma-

chine adapted only for a temporary stage—may begin
to seem negligible.

We have so far spoken only of "death" as it affects
the man whose inner confidence is in Christ, His
Character, His Values, and above all His claim to be
the expressed character of the Inexpressible God.
There is no brightly cheerful note in either the
Gospels or the rest of the New Testament for those
whose real inward trust is in their own capabilities
or in the schemes and values of the present world-
system. It is (as St. Paul insists almost *ad nauseam*)
only *"in"* Christ, *"in"* the Representative Man who
was also God, that death can be safely ignored and
"Heaven" confidently welcomed. We have no reason
to suppose that death is anything but a disaster to
those who have no grip on the timeless Life of God.

XV. THEORY INTO PRACTICE

IF A MAN accepts the fact that the Character of God
is focused in Christ, if he accepts as true the Act of
Reconciliation and the Demonstration with Death;
and if he himself is willing to abandon self-centred
living and follow the way of real living which Christ
both demonstrated and taught, he is still not out of
the wood. For he finds that apart from exceptional
effort or spasmodic resolution he is not spiritually
robust enough to live life on the new level. He simply

has not got it in him to live for long as a pioneer of the new humanity. He can see that it is right, and he can desire, even passionately, to follow the new way, but in actual practice he does not achieve this new quality of living. He may blame his own past, he may blame the ever-present effect of the God-ignoring world in which he has to live, he may even reach the melancholy conclusion that it is all a beautiful theory but that it cannot be worked in practice.

This very natural impasse was, of course, anticipated by Christ. He knew very well, for example, that the followers of His own day would very quickly collapse when the support and inspiration of His own personality were removed by death. He therefore promised them a new Spirit who should provide them with all the courage, moral reinforcement, love, patience, endurance and other qualities which they would need. A fair reading of the New Testament writings apart from the four gospels shows plainly enough that this promise was implemented. Ordinary people were not only "converted" from their previous self-loving attitude, but received sufficient spiritual vitality to cause no little stir among the world in which they lived. It is a mistake to think that in general the receiving of this gift led to excitable demonstration. Its normal function was to produce in human life the qualities which Paul catalogues in Galatians 5: love, joy, peace, patience, kindness, generosity, fidelity, adaptability, and self-control.

These are in fact the very qualities which men so easily "run short of," and which, taken together, comprise a character corresponding to the Representative Man, Christ Himself.

It is this invasion of human life by something (or Someone) from outside which the modern mind finds difficult to accept. We are all "conditioned" by the modern outlook, which regards the whole of life as a closed system. A great many things may happen inside that system, but it is unthinkable that the whole huge cause-and-effect process should in any way be interfered with from "outside."

But when we suppose, even only for the sake of argument, that the teaching of Christ is true—that this little life is acted against an immeasurable backcloth of timeless existence—it does not appear in the least impossible that under certain conditions of harmony between *this* faulty existence and *that* Perfection of Life, contact might be established. The result would be, to us, in the literal sense, supernatural. Indeed, we have already seen that a man may, even accidentally, come upon something of beauty, truth, goodness, or love, and find the "other end" is connected with the Permanent. At such times the closed-system idea is quite plainly inadequate.

Now we may wish, especially if we are more than a little tired of the closed-system idea and faintly but definitely conscious of the Real World, that these invasions might be more frequent or more demonstrable. Nevertheless, this much we do know, and can reasonably expect, that if a man honestly wants to follow the way of Christ and, as it were, opens his own personality to God, he will without any doubt receive something of the Spirit of God. As his own capacity grows and as his own channel of communication widens he will receive more. John goes so far as to call this the receiving of God's own heredity (1 John 3⁹). This does not, of course, turn a man into a spiritualist medium! The man's own real self is purified and heightened, and though he will come to bear a strong family likeness to Christ he will, paradoxically enough, be more "himself" than he was before.

We may here point out the great difference that has come to exist between the Christianity of the early days and that of today. To us it has become a performance, a keeping of rules, while to the men of those days it was, plainly, an invasion of their lives by a new quality of life altogether. The difference is due surely to the fact that we are so very slow (even though we realize our impotence) to discard the closed-system idea. We have so little of what the New Testament calls "faith." And since it is fairly obvious that "faith" is the first requisite in making contact between this and the Permanent World we can scarcely wonder at the enormous difference in quality between first-century and twentieth-century Christianity.

Without a power from outside the teaching of

Christ remains a beautiful ideal, tantalizing but un-attainable. With the closed-system sooner or later you have to say: "You can't change human nature." Ideals fail for very spiritual poverty, and cynicism and despair take their place.

But the fact of Christ's coming is itself a shattering denial of the closed-system idea which dominates our thinking. And what else is His continual advice to "have faith in God" but a call to refuse, despite all appearances, to be taken in by the closed-system type of thinking? "Ask and ye shall receive, seek and ye shall find, knock and it shall be opened unto you"—what are these famous words but an invitation to reach out for the Permanent and the Real? If we want to co-operate the Spirit is immediately available. "If ye then, for all your evil, know how to give good gifts unto your children, how much more shall your heavenly Father give the Holy Spirit to them that ask Him?"

XVI. SUMMARY

IT IS PERHAPS possible now to make a summary of the basic truths of our existence on this planet (and beyond) which can be honestly commended to meet both the facts of the situation as we can observe them, and the deep needs of the human spirit.

We can never have too big a conception of God, and the more scientific knowledge (in whatever field)

advances, the greater becomes our idea of His vast
and complicated wisdom. Yet, unless we are to remain
befogged and bewildered and give up all hope of
ever knowing God as a Person, we have to accept His
own planned focusing of Himself in a human being,
Jesus Christ.

If we accept this as fact, as *the* Fact of history, it
becomes possible to find a satisfactory and compre-
hensive answer to a great many problems, and, what
is equally important, a reasonable "shelf" on which
the unsolved perplexities may be left with every
confidence.

The "way in" to this faith is partly intellectual and
partly a matter of moral commitment. The diagnosis
of the world's sickness (and, therefore, of the individuals who comprise the world) is that the power to
love has been wrongly directed. It has either been
turned in upon itself or given to the wrong things.
The outward symptoms, and the results, of this mis-
direction are plainly obvious (at least in other people)
in what we call "sin" or "selfishness." The drastic
"conversion" which God-become-Man called for is
the reversal of the wrong attitude, the deliberate
giving of the whole power to love, first to God, and
then to other people. Without this reversal He spoke
quite bluntly of a world doomed to destruction.
Where it genuinely takes place He spoke plainly of
men being able to "know" God, to begin a new
quality of living which physical death is powerless

to touch. The three problems which this raises, (*a*) the question of *rapprochement* between the morally infected man and the Goodness of God which is automatically fatal to evil, (*b*) the question as to whether life really does continue after physical death, and (*c*) the question as to how men, even if they wish to live life on the new level, can find the power to do so—Christ solved by three demonstrations, as we have seen above.

So far we move intellectually, but we must repeat what was said in a previous chapter, that the truth of this extra-human solution to the world's impasse only comes alive when it is acted upon. The arm-chair critic must leave his arm-chair if he is to join the number of those who become convinced that here is Truth.

It appears that the strategy of Christ was to win the loyalty of the few who would honestly respond to the new way of living. They would be the pioneers of the new order, the spearhead of advance against the massed ignorance, selfishness, evil, "play-acting," and apathy of the majority of the human race. The goal which was set before them, for which they were to work and pray—and if need be, suffer and die— was the building of a new Kingdom of inner supreme loyalty, the Kingdom of God. This was to transcend every barrier of race and frontier and—and this is important—of time and space as well.

The "Church," which became the name of the

spearhead, has been, and is, open to a good deal of criticism, but it has made a great deal of hard-won progress. It is at any rate trying to carry out the divine plan, and in so far as it is working along the lines of real Truth and real Love it cannot, of course, fail—any more than God can cease to exist.

In the optimistic mid-periods between world wars some Christians talk brightly of "the earth being filled with the Knowledge of the Lord as the waters cover the sea" and of "the Kingdoms of this world becoming the Kingdom of our God and of His Christ" —as though the world-wide acceptance of the reign of God were just round the corner. This is, of course, nonsense. Those who respond to the Truth have always been a minority, and when God visited the earth in Person the response, even to Him, was not very large. Indeed it would appear that Christ (knowing how firmly evil and selfishness are entrenched and how hard it is for men to break away from their own self-love), did not anticipate a full-scale establishing of God's Kingdom on this planet even by the time when a halt was called to the experiment which we call Life (e.g. see Luke 18[8]).

The follower of the new way is therefore called to do all he can to spread "the good news of the Kingdom," but to realize at all times that the success or failure of the Kingdom can never be judged by simple reference to statistics of "Christians" at any particular time. The Kingdom is rooted in Real Life (what we sometimes call "eternity"), and as time goes on the number of those, belonging to it and taking part in its activities, but who have passed *from* the space-and-time set-up, will naturally exceed more and more the number of active members existing at any particular moment in the present world.

Critics often complain that if the world is in its present state after nineteen centuries of Christianity, then it cannot be a very good religion. They make two ridiculous mistakes. In the first place Christianity —the real thing—has never been accepted on a large scale and has therefore never been in a position to control "the state of the world," though its influence has been far from negligible. And in the second place they misunderstand the nature of Christianity. It is not to be judged by its success or failure to reform the world which rejects it. If it failed *where it is accepted* there might be grounds for complaint, but it does not so fail. It is a revelation of the true way of living, the way to know God, the way to live life of eternal quality, and is not to be regarded as a handy social instrument for reducing juvenile delinquency or the divorce rate. Any "religion," provided it can be accepted by the majority of people, can exert that sort of restrictive pressure. The religion of Jesus Christ changes people (if they are willing to pay the price of being changed) so that they quite naturally and normally live as "sons and daughters of God," and of course they exert an excellent influence on the community. But if real Christianity fails, it fails for the same reasons that Christ failed—and any condemnation rightly falls on the world which rejects both Him and it.